MELISSA HEATHERS

Dear Ego, Dear Heart

A Poetic Tale of The War Within

First published by Platypus Publishing 2024

Copyright © 2024 by Melissa Heathers

All rights reserved. No part of this publication may be reproduced, stored or transmitted in any form or by any means, electronic, mechanical, photocopying, recording, scanning, or otherwise without written permission from the publisher. It is illegal to copy this book, post it to a website, or distribute it by any other means without permission.

This novel is entirely a work of fiction. The names, characters and incidents portrayed in it are the work of the author's imagination. Any resemblance to actual persons, living or dead, events or localities is entirely coincidental.

Melissa Heathers asserts the moral right to be identified as the author of this work.

Melissa Heathers has no responsibility for the persistence or accuracy of URLs for external or third-party Internet Websites referred to in this publication and does not guarantee that any content on such Websites is, or will remain, accurate or appropriate.

Designations used by companies to distinguish their products are often claimed as trademarks. All brand names and product names used in this book and on its cover are trade names, service marks, trademarks and registered trademarks of their respective owners. The publishers and the book are not associated with any product or vendor mentioned in this book. None of the companies referenced within the book have endorsed the book.

First edition

ISBN: 978-1-965016-39-8

Cover art by Moko Heathers

*This book was professionally typeset on Reedsy.
Find out more at reedsy.com*

Acknowledgments
To my chosen family and friends: without your presence in my life, the war between my ego and my heart would still rage on.
To my soul sister, who has fostered my creativity and supported the light within me – your love is cherished in an unbreakable sisterly bond.
To the collective: keep faith in yourself and allow your heart to guide you.

Contents

Preface	iii
Acknowledgments	iv
Introduction	1

I Part One - Pure Light

1	Chapter 1 - Love is Born, Love is Loss	7
2	Chapter 2 - Once Love is Lost, War Comes Shortly After	13
3	Chapter 3 - The Hardships of Life	16
4	Chapter 4 - Our War Torn Reality	19
5	Chapter 5 - The War is Real	25
6	Chapter 6 - The Commander	32
7	Chapter 7 - War is On The Brink	35
8	Chapter 8 - Fear of Faith or Fight For Faith	38
9	Chapter 9 - Trust in Our Love or Doubt Life	41
10	Chapter 10 - Value Love or Desire Ego	44
11	Chapter 11 - A Fight Without a Cause	48

II Part 2 - The War Begins

12	Chapter 12 - All War Starts With the Inner Dialog	57
13	Chapter 13 - Declaration Of Mind War	61
14	Chapter 14 - Rally The Troops	66

15	Chapter 15 - The Enemies Are Coming Near and Far	72
16	Chapter 16 - The Battlefield	78
17	Chapter 17 - Fighting For Our Deadly Sins	83
18	Chapter 18 - Enduring The War	88
19	Chapter 19 - The Wall of Protection	90
20	Chapter 20 - The Inner War	94
21	Chapter 21	101
22	Chapter 22 - Waging War Out of Love or Die in Fear	104
23	Chapter 23 - Trusting The Battle	107

III PART 3 - Ending The War and The Aftermath

24	Chapter 24 - Impose Gratitude on Thy Enemy	113
25	Chapter 25 - Despair in a World of War	117
26	Chapter 26 - Talk to Each Part of Ourselves with Gentle...	122
27	Chapter 27 - Embodying a Truce Within	128
28	Chapter 28 - Embracing Our Truth	131
29	Chapter 29 - The Shift Within	135
30	Chapter 30 - Holding Space Until We Are Home	138
31	Chapter 31 - Welcome Home	142

Preface

The internal struggle is a fierce battle
    It represents the response to our soul
    The rise and fall of our own empire
    Enduring pain inflicted by the weapons of conflict
    We seek to mend our wounds through the love that resides within

Acknowledgments

I would like to thank my cover designer, Moko Heathers. Her creativity fuels me to remain inspired to become the best version of myself.

I would also like to thank my publishing company Platypus Publishing, their unique way of support was truly a blessing to look at my story from a different perspective.

Introduction

Dear Ego, Dear Heart
Introduction:

From the dawn of history there have been wars within humankind, combat between humans and the strife that lies within us. Unless mankind learns to disarm themselves from the battle between the ego and the heart, war of all types will always exist.

We are all born pure and innocent with only the consciousness of light and love. As infants and children, we know nothing of darkness and hate, it is unconscious at the beginning of life, but the shadow grows bigger as we grow with life. Our trauma, adversity and outside influences during our lifetime generates darkness and dims our light within.

Once darkness appears, sometimes we get stoic in it for what may seem to be a lifetime. As our darkness evolves, our inner flame smolders. Our obscurity will latch onto the certainty of others and the faith in uncertainty we are meant to endure turns to fear. Through life we learn to believe that certainty is our truth and our trust in ourselves is hidden in the shadows. The truth of who we really are is lost to the validity of others and outside influences.

The wickedness of trauma generates vicious patterns and our patterns become our infinity. We circle them endlessly in a cycle of self-destruction. The more our mind recycles the carbon copies the more the ego grows and becomes combative towards feelings and who we authentically are. In this clash between the mind and heart we start splintering away from our true self and the division of selves begins. Eventually, our conflicting feelings and thoughts of despair wage war within us.

Outside influences show us unwanted behaviours, our beliefs and values are learnt from a tainted society. It becomes a game of tug of war of who we are and what someone else wants us to be. In our world of war with false beliefs, unhealthy behaviour, and social conditioning we eventually lose ourselves. Our wholeness gets segregated into our two selves: the ego and the heart.

The ego lives from pride and fear, it wants control and power. The heart lives from a place of love. When the self-splits into these two parts, the bias war starts to brew in mind. The ego will strive at any cost, even war to stay separated from the heart so it can remain in an illusion of control. Being strayed from love will be the ego's mission.

Once a strayed our self-identity is lost in the wishes of the world not the wishes of our heart. Being lost in who we are creates doubt and annihilating thoughts, we are hidden in shame and shine in self-destruction. While lost our ego remains closed and predictable, usually trapped in an abolishing mindset. Our Heart remains open, but our light is hidden in darkness until it's time to come home to ourselves and shine again.

Like war, our two selves can stray away from each other and fight each other for years, sometime decades. In our separation we get hurt, we get hardened, and we lose touch with who we really are. Parts of our life are lost to battle and sorrow but keep faith that our authentic self grows from adversity and love prevails from our sorrow and grief. Only despair can break our barriers that have been placed from our inner and outer wars. Eventually our light and love that is buried deep within the concrete of life, will be ready to illuminate the cracks.

Once the barriers are broken, love seeps through the cracks filling the murk with light. As the light gently sweeps through us, we slowly break open and shine once again. Once love illuminates our ego's darkness, life is whole, and light enters once again.

During our inner war, we deviate from our heart in the name of love, led by pride of the commander, the ego. The war we endure eventually will lead us home again to our pure and peaceful state of being.

I

Part One - Pure Light

1

Chapter 1 - Love is Born, Love is Loss

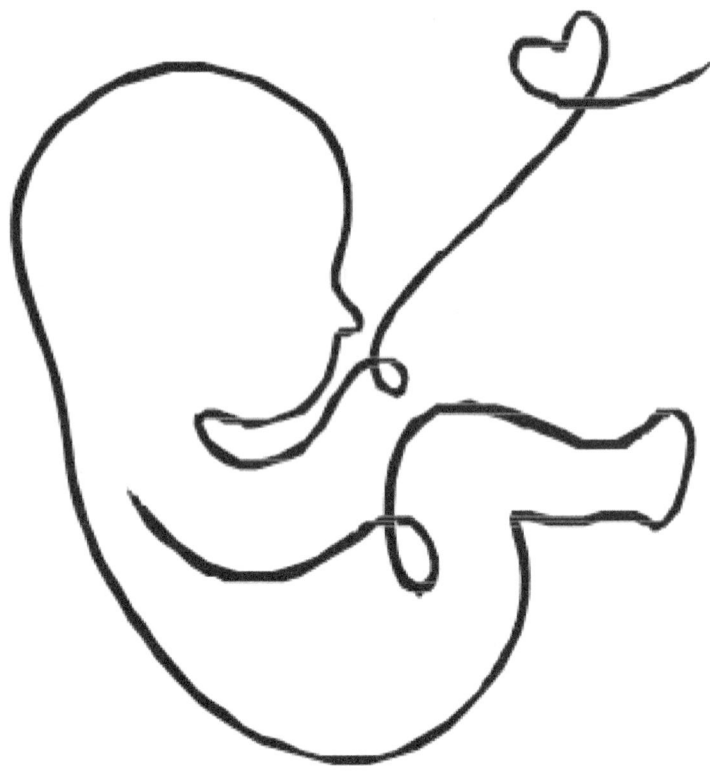

Dear Ego,

A bundle of joy is born and that bundle is us. We are born pure and innocent and we only know love and light. We are unaware of good or evil. We are naive to ego and only radiate love.

Dear Heart,

We are born as humankind but we live in a world with darkness and light. Eventually our light smolders and our innocence is lost to the corruption of the world. Our purity becomes controlled by our impurities of the mind and life takes a toll on us. Eventually the influence of the outside world influences our inner world. It is just a matter of time before our mind becomes impure from the darkness of the world we exist in.

Dear Ego,

We are born in human form in a world with a lot of darkness but our journey on earth starts with the blessings of being created as pure light and love. Outside influences eventually distort our reality and we are led into despair. While in despair remember it does not matter how much absence of light there is in our life, love can always be found to lead us out of our gloom.

Dear Heart,

Once our soul is manifested into human form, then life becomes cursed by ego. Humanity is cruel and we are at the mercy of our experiences and influences. Many of us thrive in doom and only survive in the suffering of life because that is what we are born into. It is what we know.

Dear Ego,

During our life we are meant to experience pain, live in darkness, and feel despair. Our adversities are part of our journey to make us turn away from ourselves, only to force us to learn to trust our process. Keep faith that what we endure in life it will eventually lead us back to our heart's center.

Dear Heart,

Despair is the darkest part of mind, while suffering here there are no gimps of light. While in melancholy we are detached from our ego and our heart. The voices of the ego go unheard and the love in our heart cannot be felt because all hope is lost.

Dear Ego,

While here keep, faith the heaviness of dejection will lift because our unconditional love that is being weighed down by the hurt is strong enough to hold space and heal the pain.

Dear Heart,

Even when the hurt lifts, the inner conflict will still exist. The ego is prideful, and it does not want to show weakness. Our pride fuels our thoughts and attaches to our hurt as a catalysis to wage war within ourselves.

Dear Ego,

There are many parts of us that lead us down a path of self-destruction, not just pride. Too much self-praise can cause harm to both parts of us too. Our mind gets preserved in the praise we give to ourselves, and our heart gets tarnished from too much pride of the stuck mind. Knowing our worth and having humility can be diplomatic and keep us free from war.

Dear Heart,

Ego centrism and pride keep the commander strong and in control.

Dear Ego,

Our mind only perceives pride as strength but at the root it is rotten. Pride is deceiving and it is neglectful to both the mind and the heart. It is self-righteous and shields us from the truth of the outer and inner world in which we exist.

Dear Heart,

Pride is what makes our defenses strong, when the ego converses with our pride we think we are loved.

Dear Ego,

It is only a hindrance to our authenticity because it is disguised as love but really, it is conceited. Pride has no version of love but rather a defense tactic to keep us from the best version of ourselves. It is a comparison to others with low self-esteem. Being humble is real love to the self and others.

Dear Heart,

The ego is ready to fight for pride and wants to know we are loved in any facet.

Dear Ego,

Know that all of us are loved. Listen to your heart and know the facet of love from pride is an illusion. Prestige only destroys anything in its way, including us in any state of being we are in. Embracing humility is the real facet of love. Being down to earth can get us through our adversity, egotism will only cause more self-destruction.

Dear Heart,

A mindful of superiority during any hardship can fight the war we are facing.

Dear Ego,

We can only battle our inner wars with love, not self-inflation. Using arrogance as our defenses will set us up for failure because it is not a true reflection of who we really are. Pride is fear and nothing is ever won in fear.

Dear Heart,

Love is born and love is lost in the deepest conversations we have with ourselves. We learn to accept what we hear about ourselves. We are brainwashed in believing the narratives we tell ourselves and we are shaped by the perception that others have about us.

Dear Ego,

Love always exists and is never lost, even when we are lost in the conditioning bestowed upon us in our life. While lost, our heart knows fear is lack of faith and pride is the lack of faith in ourselves.

Dear Heart,

What weighs in our mind will always be vastly different from what weighs in our heart.

Dear Ego,

When love is lost in our mind our heart will give loving kindness to our heavy thoughts because we are born as love and love will always exist within us, it can never be castaway in war.

2

Chapter 2 - Once Love is Lost, War Comes Shortly After

Dear Heart,

When our ego has abolished any loving thoughts, then our ego will be quick to sense the tethered bias and will latch onto this weakness within with armed forces.

Dear Ego,

The core of us never wants to fight with the mind. It tries to send loving thoughts and positive affirmations. Inner war is never a desire of the heart. Authenticity wants to deflate our ego and be in a peaceful state with the mind, not in a war-torn state of being.

Dear Heart,

Our inflated sense of self identifies with the mind better than the heart. Our egotism wants to maintain a sense of control. It is motivated to justify our cognitive function and thinks it is worth will be found the bloodshed of our self-love.

Dear Ego,

Remember in the annihilation, nothing is within our control. Trying to be in control of our own mind is like being a prisoner of war. We will only find hurt from unmet expectations and sorrow in the illusion of control. Our current state of mind is altered by the world's expectations of who it wants us to be. If we can learn to observe our thoughts instead of trying to control them, then our life will not have inner war, only love and peace.

Dear Heart,

Our ego is selfish and wants to be the ruler of our land. The commander's job is to dictate and defeat the heart with no empathy. The ego cannot remain satisfied and proud if there is more than one commander of the land.

Dear Ego,

Our heart shutters at the feelings of having conflict within us. Our loving heart wants to avoid a royal battle, but our soul knows that each part of us has perspective. Our heart will not interrogate the inner thoughts of our mind but rather show it humility and lead our defenses with loving kindness on the battlefield.

Dear Heart,

The id's armour is strong, it is made from environment, toxic relationships, criticism, experiences, and genetics. Standing up to it will drain our source to defeat it on the war-field.

Dear Ego,

Our source can withstand any armed conflict because it is intangible and infinite. It has endurance of million troops and the resilience to rise to any occasion for love to prevail.

Dear Heart,

Once love is lost in our mind, the soldiers come marching in to start the lifelong war.

Dear Ego,

Long battles may puncture and hurt the heart, but our self-love and respect will always stand up to the armor of the ego. Love never dies in any war; it can only ever be buried deep among the ashes. Even after the aftermath of war, love will be felt from the ashes of our burnt soul.

3

Chapter 3 - The Hardships of Life

Dear Heart

Facing life is extremely difficult, especially when many of our life experiences and hardships have led the mind and heart into war. Within the inner battle we are our own worst enemy and our ego has grown to be an egotistical commander who wants to win the quarrel at any cost.

Dear Ego,

Life's journey will march us straight to hell and back but during our travels within us we will find the strength to endure and the resilience to continue marching through our most difficult trenches. At the end of the disciplined march and once out of the trenches, we will find our peace.

Dear Heart,

Many times in our lifetime, we frontier down dark ditches with no glimpse of light. When we cannot see the light at the end of the tunnel and that is when we lose hope. There is only so much one person can endure before our suffering keeps us in the ravines of destruction.

Dear Ego,

Self-destruction is the sacrifice required in our life, so we can create new life once again. Only from the ashes of our pain can we rise again new and in love with who we are.

Dear Heart,

Among the rubble, love is hard to find. Self-destruction causes cognitive dissonance. In our brokenness self-ego thrives because it is the part of us that rationalizes what we think. Being egocentric allows our thoughts to weigh heavy on our mind to persist in war. We process intrusive thoughts and spin them to the worst-case scenarios so they can beat us down, while we are stuck in them.

Dear Ego,

Our heart will always feel the pain of our inner conflict and hardships. The desire to have harmony within will inevitably guide us through our broken shards of life. These broken peaces give us the strength to take a leap of faith that we can trust the uncertainty of life's imbalance to lead us to a place of balance.

Dear Heart,

Our deprivations have caused us to splinter from each other and war has veered its ugly head keeping us segregated. Our ego's perception views life in a negative light and thinks all love is lost to darkness in our cruel world. We believe balance is only how we perceive it exists in the consciousness of our mind and not our heart.

Dear Ego,

Suffering is growth within. The injustice of our unnecessary pain is the only battle that can bring us back home to ourselves. The war we have within ourselves is where love and light are found once again to bring harmony between our ego and heart.

Dear Heart,

The war within us is real. Our ego, the commander, will always fight for the justice we perceive in this conscious life.

Dear Ego,

Yes, the conflict within us is real with a deep purpose. Our heart, the king, will always stand for freedom from our self-inflicted slavery. The king knows love is the foundation that we all evolve from. We also know in our heart that the illusions of our intellectual capabilities we currently stand for have no purpose and only generate war because we do not know a different reality yet. Our soul wants to bring our purpose to life in a new reality.

4

Chapter 4 - Our War Torn Reality

Dear Heart,
 We live in a war-torn reality and not an illusion.

Dear Ego,
 Our hub is our reality, and we need to coexist together. You often live in your own reality creating a tampered trajectory for us. The curve in the trajectory is strong and leads us down many bumpy trails. It is a difficult journey down many roads and paths of chaos.

Dear Heart,
 Our mind is meant to change the trajectory of life, and our thoughts are meant to carve who we become. Any journey is meant to have many directions and realities. Our direction on the path of life is created from our beliefs from the real world and the world we exists in is torn.

Dear Ego,
 Existing only in the outside world that is already in conflict is

challenging but we do not need to have war-torn reality within us. We are the force that can move us along our path within the same space and in peace. We can march in parallel with each other and not be at crossroads with the two side of us.

Dear Heart,

Our state of mind always distorts our existence because it is how we survive in the chaos of life. We have lived through hell; trauma, illness, death, neglect, and abuse. It has been tragic but this is the reality we know. We have learnt to believe this is what we deserve and what we are worth. It is our normal state of being.

Dear Ego,

Life is meant to have traveling hardships to find the right direction back home to us. Difficulties are meant to guide us to our life's purpose. All our pain is the driving force to find unconditional love within. We need the difficulties of life moments to find our worth.

Dear Heart,

We are triggered by our trauma. We learn to believe we deserve the abuse and that we are worthless. Negligence creates isolation and loneliness. Tragically in our greif our mind keeps cycling in negative emotions from our loss and the things we have endured.

Dear Ego,

Instead of creating our divide when we experience disturbing events, we can grow together, beats being at war. Difficult experiences leave us feeling unsafe, but we can find safety within us through courage. When we suffer cruelty from others, we are given the opportunity to find our self-love. When we are not cared for by the people who are supposed to love us, we can learn to care for ourselves. When we feel lonely and isolated, we can connect to our source within. When we have a loss, we can feel the emotions and hold space for them while moving through it. Not all our trauma needs to be the source of our internal conflict, it can also be the event that brings internal peace.

Dear Heart

In our state of being it is hard to find courage, we thrive in our suffering, and we only know cruelty to our spirit. We neglect our soul because neglect is familiar, we isolate ourselves to shelter our depression, and we disconnect from life, so we do not have to feel any emotions. This way of being is our war-torn reality.

Dear Ego,

Living life constantly on the battlefield is fear driven but if we learn that our fear is meant to frighten us to find strength and teach us resilience, we do not need to live in war. Our distress gives our life purpose, and the disregard of our life reveals our life.

Dear Heart,

Our war-torn reality knows no difference. This mind's reality is stuck in the hardships of life and the suffering they have caused us. Egotism thrives in a torn state of being. It is the war of our belief system that we were taught and not the values of our truth that we want to know.

Dear Ego,

The truth will always set us free. One can accept anything if the truth is heard. Our truth is our freedom. Our rationale is not our truth. Our rationale is our mind's voice. Sometimes we get stuck in our voice of reason. We believe our reason over the faith from our heart.

Dear Heart,

How does one find the truth? When we are always listening to reason and stuck in our own heads. We learnt from an early age that the world's reality is our truth and we need to defend it at any cost.

Dear Ego,

When finding truth, listen to your heart by feeling it. Be open to what you are feeling. Our heart is the center and the wisdom. It is our life force and only speaks our wisdom. Admitting our principle can be difficult but it is better than being at war with ourselves.

Dear Heart,

Our state of mind is good at altering our feelings or suppressing them so that they are silenced. Getting to know and accepting our feelings is a new state of being and it requires a mind shift. Our mind only shifts to protect what makes it think it is secure and certain off. We are certain that by beating ourselves up we are secure. We think we are secure when there is a divide between us.

Dear Ego,

The heart has felt many beatings but to get to the heart of

the matter and mend it, our thoughts need to align with our feelings. By listening to our heart, it will bring us joy because within us we know our worth. Our soul knows what we really want and gives us empathy and compassion. Our worth and authenticity is worth honoring instead of bleeding it out from bloodshed on the battle front.

Dear Heart,

The matters of the heart are in the middle of a renegade. The heart has been deserted by the mind many times because our mind does not know how to be loyal to the heart. The path of less resistance is marching to the war front and wants a crusade of the soul.

Dear Ego,

Ego may not always be loyal, but our heart is loyal to all parts of who we are. You may desert our cause, but love will never desert our principle.

Dear Heart

We desert our heart because quickly after we are born our light is lost and life gets real. Life traumas submerge and produce a dark rippling of inner conflicts. These conflicts become our identity and destroy our authenticity and any unconditional love we once had for ourselves.

Dear Ego,

The heaviness we endure in life is only part of our legitimacy. Embracing love while we go through difficulties of our tides is our absolute light and that can never be lost to any deep wave of life. Our ripples eventually turn into waves and our waves roll into ripples on the shoreline. The only way through the challenges of life's waves is with love. If we look at a wave what we should see is energy travelling as one force where the base is dark and heavy while the tip is translucent and light. There is no separation or battle within the body of water, just cohesive movement within the energy.

5

Chapter 5 - The War is Real

Dear Heart,

The war within is real and the divide between our two selves is our reality of existence. Our mind is armed with many weapons; tanks, guns, and bombs ready to defend our current reality.

Dear Ego,

War does not need to exist just gentle loving kindness towards our truth. The weapons you hold inside your mind can be disarmed. Love conquers all to live in peace with all parts of us. Truth wants to set us free from our rivalry.

Dear Heart,

Truth is what creates war. The truth is our reality and is represented by us with limited beliefs, deceit, and hate. We become what we surround ourselves with and eventually we believe what we hear. Our behaviors are taught in the disheartening world of so-called truth.

Dear Ego,

The unpleasant facts are not decided by the outside world. Certainty is the spirit within us and it is subjective not objective. It is our wisdom; it is our knowing and it is our longing. Our reality is within our soul not the concerns of the outer world. There is never war within a loving soul, only the ego believes that the war is real.

Dear Heart,

Our pride makes the war real so we can continue to exist in the reality of the society in which we exist. Our complacency is based on reality. Ego fears knowing our authenticity. The mind is truth and our knowledge is what makes us wise and it fights to be right. Human existence is generated from the world that surrounds us.

Dear Ego,

When we only listen to the words of others and not the words from our heart, the mind will create turmoil within because most times other opinions go against our values. Destruction will prevail when we start believing in the things we see and hear. War will become real when we do not keep faith in what we know in our heart.

Dear Heart,

The turmoil between the mind and heart sometimes is a lifelong battle. It is the war of dark and light. Attacks in darkness are favorable to the outcome of the ego because we are at our strongest in our night thoughts. Many times, the war halts at dawn and we sleepwalk during the day to keep peace in the world around us by doing what is expected of us.

CHAPTER 5 - THE WAR IS REAL

Dear Ego,

Sieges during the dusk hours are for good reason. In the absence of light, the source is less visible but awakens again with the brightness of the dawn.

Dear Heart,

During the darkest hours, the attacker can exploit and be in combat with the heart. Thoughts of hate are from fear but self-destruction in the witching hour is a cruel battle.

Dear Ego,

Shame becomes our gloomy thoughts in the late hours of the day. It is hidden within self-destruction and becomes our demise. We can learn to nurture shame instead of fighting it and hating ourselves because of it.

Dear Heart,

Shame is what we know. We live in a shameful world and society has shamed us our whole life. From this shame, we learned to shame ourselves. Our beliefs believe we are shameful, and that self-humiliation is part of us. Rationally, learning to unlearn this learned behavior seems impossible. Our mind has already internalized our stigma, and it has brought civil war between our mind and heart.

Dear Ego,

The war is not lost. We can learn humility from our humiliation. We can take honor from our shame and teach self-respect. Practicing self-love can end the war within, we can become constructive instead of destructive.

Dear Heart,

The ID runs from love and gravitates towards the troops on battlefield. The conflict is comforting in the mind. We believe the negativity and take pleasure in the strokes of our ego. Our bullets of self-doubt keeps the war zone real. The fight towards our heart is real, and our thoughts generate it.

Dear Ego,

The heart is conflicted from our thoughts and feels the battles deeply. The fight is real but if we can learn to accept the love within, the war can cease fire towards us.

Dear Heart,

I never think of healing the war wounds from society with love because all I know is combat to protect our beliefs. To fight is all we know in our mind, and we perceive the fight as real.

Dear Ego,

The battle will always be real, it is a part of us, but our loving heart wants to embrace our challenging thoughts with gentle kindness to generate peace not war.

Dear Heart,

Beating ourselves up is so natural to us because we have become hypersensitive to our thoughts. Peace is lost in these bullying notions. Kindness is barricaded behind the blows of disservice.

Dear Ego,

Self-abuse is taught at an early age, and we naturally embrace it to cope with trauma and neglect. But self-compassion can also be embraced. Allow the ego to receive compassion, so the war between the two selves can cease to exist.

Dear Heart,
The power struggle between our mind and heart is real. The conflict starts early in life. How can the two self's have unity when the war has been real our whole life?

Dear Ego,
The effects of our lifelong war cause us so much grief. The core of us feels all the real pain of our combat and it feels like the ego is trying to compel our free will; this hurts our heart so deeply.

Dear Heart,
Full control is the mind's aim. It wants to know it is in full control and the heart is powerless. Ensuring the war stays real is our ego's mission.

Dear Ego,
Our love knows the war between us is real, it is the part of us that nurtures the hurt. The heart is the most powerful part of us because it holds the love to heal our battle wounds. It gives us grace, acceptance, peace, and joy. Compassion accepts all parts of us with grace and ceasefire to our combative mind and peace to our soul.

Dear Heart,
Our thoughts fight strongly with vicious attacks to the heart. Oftentimes gunshots destroy our emotions. They are powerful in the reality of war because they rationalize what we observe,

keep things real and desensitize us. Our thoughts are trained like soldiers to the world's values and comply to what we are told. We want our heart to be complainant too.

Dear Ego,

Our empathy unconditionally understands that negative notions are forced upon us and rooted deeply but our grace can give our mind relief. Oftentimes our heart suffers from what we rationalize but often our suffering brings our calm to the inner war.

Dear Heart,

Ego fights for pride to keep our power and control. It wants to be a free thinker; it believes the only way to still be prideful is to keep the attacks harsh and the strife going.

Dear Ego,

Our heart feels how much the ego yearns for power and how our pride consumes us. To be free, we must end the separation between us and align as one. In our wholeness we are liberated and living true to ourselves with mind, body, and soul. Accepting the heart's space in the mind will give passage to free thoughts from a place of love.

Dear Heart,

Full transparency, our belief system controls the ego, and we want victory and the throne

Dear Ego,

The throne is only a part of the kingdom, but love is the true ruler. Love can hold space while in refuge, and it can sit silent while other parts of us try to rule our land, but the real kingdom is love.

Dear Heart,

On our battlefront, the purpose of the fight is to allow our ego to dethrone love's power over the kingdom.

Dear Ego,

Our riches are only found within, and the crown of victory is the love we have for ourselves and others. In our life it is necessary to rise and fight against ourselves to find a new beginning and rebuild our kingdom. In the destruction of our palace, war is where we find self-love and the strength to rebuild from the rubble left in the aftermath of the war. During the reconstruction of our life we are united, find ourselves and become whole.

Chapter 6 - The Commander

Dear Heart,

When the two selves are divided there are two commanders within us, rising together united is a conflict of interest. Our egotism wants to remain as the ruler of mind, while our love wants to rule our heart.

Dear Ego,

The mind's commander rules with negativity and desires control like a fearful narcissist. Our heart only leads our soul from a place of love. The only command of the heart is faith and with faith we can let go of control.

Dear Heart

Our thoughts are driven by ego and our combative actions are in response to our thoughts. We lash out and attack because the commander is responding to the fear of loss of control.

Dear Ego,

Serving our highest self and good can only be led from the kingdom of love and directed by the King. The palace of the heart is free from pride, arrogance, and limited beliefs.

Dear Heart,

Our head space holds a lot of authority. Its alarming thoughts can distract us enough and splinter us from our center. It is ranked powerful enough to segregate our mind, body, and spirit, causing detachment.

Dear Ego,

Having the notion that our limited beliefs are stronger than the power of love is how the war starts within ourselves and in humankind. Our worthless thoughts break us down and cast doubt about who we are. Not wanting to accept ourselves in our entirety hurts our heart like an explosion in war injuring innocent people.

Dear Heart,

The commander is cruel towards us and it has is been trained to stir up a fight. It is all the commander knows what to do. The command in the mind is to always find a way to break us down. We will continue to punish ourselves to commence an inner battle in hopes to keep control of what is familiar to us.

Dear Ego,

Self-cruelty is oppressive, the love within will lead us out of our darkest war and the king will have mercy on our commanders' hurtful tactics.

Dear Heart,

The headman's strength grows every day from support of deadly notions. We are forcibly influenced by the outside world. The head flexes when forced to acknowledge the land treaties and takes pride in knowing it affects the kings core. The inner dialog within the mind makes the inner conflict survive, preparing for battle is the heart's only possibility because war will always exist.

Dear Ego,

The reality of our war is just the tip of the iceberg. Beneath the surface is a hidden body of problems that desires being explored. The depths of us wants the mind to delve underneath the surface and have an encounter with what is hidden in the body of water. Experiencing life together can bring us closer and stop any war from even beginning.

Chapter 7 - War is On The Brink

Dear Heart,

Many parts of us will always remain hidden. The purpose of a surprise attack is to keep our authenticity hidden and it is the mission of the mind. There is glory in the ego winning the inner battle; it keeps the mind's fragments at the tip of the iceberg while keeping the actual problems submerged beneath the surface. This is a cause worth fighting for.

Dear Ego,

Beneath the surface is where the beauty lies. Our depth is endless if you take the opportunity to explore instead of wage war. Our heart would love for the mind to embrace the unknown and delve deeply into the dark submerged waters of life. In the depths we will find wisdom. Our interrelated parts of each other can share the wisdom instead of fighting over it

Dear Heart,

Our mind fears the depths of the heart immersed in the dark

water. Ego pridefully fights on top of the iceberg in the certainty of being on top.

Dear Ego,
Never fear diving in. What is found underneath the surface in the unknown is worth exploring. The vastness of depth is limitless. The knowledge of the mind will observe, while transcendence will blow our mind. The beauty found within can open the mind to a world of opportunities instead of remaining closed-minded and staying defensive.

Dear Heart,
We have been taught that it is safer to keep our vulnerabilities hidden in the depths.

Dear Ego,
Our vulnerability is our strength, and it needs to rise to the surface. Our heart will lash out with self-love to allow vulnerability to be seen.

Dear Heart,
The priority of the ego will always try to withstand the shifting iceberg. Ego's faith is in the tip and our fear is below the surface.

Dear Ego,
The tip is just a small part of us and does not even scratch the surface of the whole iceberg. The more we fear and neglect below the surface, the colder we become. But the heart is always warm and will eventually crack the ice to surface and fight for love. Our faith in love will peacefully battle our fear so inclusion of ourselves can rise.

CHAPTER 7 - WAR IS ON THE BRINK

Dear Heart,

Fear in the mind of losing control of their stance will always fight to keep the body of the iceberg submerged in the frozen dark water.

8

Chapter 8 - Fear of Faith or Fight For Faith

Dear Ego,

Fight to regain trust in faith. Our mind will always have control but allowing faithful thoughts to enter the mind space will bring peace and not war to both parts of us.

Dear Heart,

Our ego only stays in control by filling our thoughts with fear. Words of doubt, untruth and hate keep us locked up like prisoners of civil war.

Dear Ego

Even while imprisoned the heart still beats with love. It is the part of us that will keep our faith alive. Glimpse of trust, truth and tenderness will always linger by the prison door. Only faith can free us while we suffer through our imprisonment.

Dear Heart,

Every day we live in conflict, and we are prey to the notion of fearing ourselves. What is in our head keeps the war waging during all irrational and rational thoughts.

Dear Ego,
Being prey is part of human existence, but faith allows one to resist the attack. Having kindness towards our irrational thoughts will allow rational notions to disarm themselves. It will give us love instead of self-harm.

Dear Heart,
The darkest parts of our ego always perceive any threats as harm and lack faith. The ID is self-deprecating, self-harming and self-blaming. It believes we are unworthy and has thoughts of guilt when we think we are worthy of ourselves.

Dear Ego,
Keep faith that we will rise from any depth and any hesitant part of us because our love knows no depth and it knows no fear. Know that our authentic self is enough and that our soul is beautiful. Believe in the power of our love and that it is strong enough to break the barricades of our war. Once our walls are destroyed, we will be whole and have order once again.

Dear Heart,
If our light rids our darkness, then our ego will cease to exist and only our authentic self will shine. This part of us would be lost to our soul.

Dear Ego,
Our ego will always exist but once aligned it will exist differ-

ently. The divide between us would be gone, along with our animosity. We would exist as one and not the two separate selves.

Both of us would have access to our self-love and self-control. We would be empowered and thrive, not be stuck in our punishment and destruction of the violence. Do not fear the light, trust it because it loves all of us.

Dear Heart,

Shedding shadows with illumination is terrifying. Thoughts of it alone trigger an inner bloodshed in the mind. Trusting our radiance to shine creates a sense of doubt because the ego does not know how to be bright and cheery. It has been taught gloom and oppression. It only knows violence and self-destruction.

Dear Ego,

Do not doubt who we are but rather be devoted to all sides of us. Embrace our conviction. Be selfless, not hostile. The rage we think we need to keep is only our fear. It will always keep us as a prisoner of war.

Chapter 9 - Trust in Our Love or Doubt Life

Dear Heart,

Our life experiences have created doubt within us. The uncertainty keeps the mind games flushing in a lifetime of internal conflict. Suffering is our trusted certainty.

Dear Ego,

Believe that our life's journey is meant to be challenging. Without pain there could be no faith that you were always meant to have. Know we will be okay with the person we are. Certainty comes from trusting yourself and the faith that you can endure the hardships of life and that within these difficulties resilience is found.

Dear Heart,

Adversity and doubt keep us stuck in a raging war amongst ourselves. Lack of worship keeps us certain that we need the great divide. Survival of the fittest is our mantra and our mind wants to remain fit to win the war, so we do not doubt our life.

Dear Ego,

The gift of adversity is endurance. If there is trust, we will know with certainty that this too shall pass and the war within will end. Our heart has no doubt in the life we were given and our admiration for life limits the doubt we feel.

Dear Heart,

Our ego's doubt is strong enough to protest any change. Knowing how to embrace thoughts without judgment instead of tormenting us seems impossible. Our mental picture is brawny with confidence when it can humiliate our soul.

Dear Ego,

The heart's most robust emotion is love. Our reverence is entrusted to seize our darkest thoughts without passing judgment on them. Naturally and with ease self-regard can abolish self-inflicted torment. Through gentle loving kindness the shackles of our fear can be released.

Dear Heart,

Self-doubt generates resistance to accept change. Our suspicion of love motivates us to stay stuck in the inner war because we fear what may come if we surrender.

Dear Ego,

Trust that acceptance is the key to change. Know that change is growth. Humankind is not meant to stay stuck in war, we are meant to evolve as one. Only within surrender can we come back home to our authentic self.

CHAPTER 9 - TRUST IN OUR LOVE OR DOUBT LIFE

Dear Heart,

Our heart center is the ego's enemy. Our socially conditioned notions have difficulty being submissive to the idea of evolving as one. Our fight response is certainty in our uncertainty.

Dear Ego,

Trust that all parts of us are worthy of love not war. Keep faith and do not doubt the love we have within us. It is always there even if our mind does not know it yet.

Dear Heart,

We exist in a guilted society, and this creates doubt and unworthiness in so many. We are shamed and judged by others for being our authentic self. The shame we know cast dark and deep thoughts of doubt. Shame is so powerful we are willing to wage war within to protect the true self from ever being seen. In our mind, not being exposed in a cruel shaming society is worth the battle.

Dear Ego,

Instead of war and hiding in shame, know it is okay to show the world our authenticity, never be unsure about who we really are. Who we are is nothing to feel guilty about. Guilt only weighs heavy on our mind, not in our heart. Never doubt the power of love but rather value it.

10

Chapter 10 - Value Love or Desire Ego

Dear Heart,

Our ego does not doubt the value of love, rather it fears it because it knows the strength of the heart. Our ego desires total control so our values do not take over and our beliefs stay in power. The desire is so strong it brings war upon us, the mind versus the heart. The battle of the unconscious versus the conscious.

Dear Ego,

Our character needs to feel things, not just think and believe the things others have told us are true. Knowing and feelings can exist in harmony. We can only validate our desires by having feelings about them. We can only evolve our values by having desires. We feel what we want, and we learn what is important in life. The irony is that desire is part of ego and value is from our heart. It is not meant to be warfare; it needs to be a loving embrace.

CHAPTER 10 - VALUE LOVE OR DESIRE EGO

Dear Heart,

Our state of mind craves power over self-harmony because we know how powerful authenticity is. Expectation is our minds war and to achieve what is expected is a desire of the ego.

Dear Ego,

Being authentic is strength but it is only powerful when we value and accept our entirety. Mind, body and soul are the fabric of who we really are. It makes up our values, our desires, our emotions, our feelings, our thoughts, our faith, and our dreams. Authenticity does fight against any part of us it is only inclusive of all of us. It values love.

Dear Heart

Life has taught us ego possesses and desires: unworthiness, shame, fear, loathing, greed, and negativity. These desires pull and they often own our mind, keeping us in a constant state of internal conflict. Our authenticity is hidden in the shadow of what controls the commander. Ego does not value love, it rejects it and when our soul tries to shine, desire takes over, keeping us stuck in constant power struggle.

Dear Ego,

The heart possesses and values: worth, honor, calmness, positivity, and love. Our values are influential, and they own the joy in our heart. Our love is our authenticity sometimes in the shadow but always valued by the light.

Dear Heart,

I am the part of you that is driven by fear. Fear desires to be comfortable in our skin and prevents us from taking the risk of letting love in. Fear ignores the whispers of our heart to avert any change in life. Fear is a part of ego, and our ego is destructive. It wages emotional violence against us to stay living in a constant state of fear.

Dear Ego,

I am the part of you that is love. Our love values our faith and endures adversity in the risk we take. Our values drive our soul's desires for purpose, and we would love for our ego to feel the beauty of the soul, so we can stop living in fear and desire love. We only ever take risk from a place of love. Our heart will only ever comfort our fears and lead us from faith through change. When in a good place, coming from the right intentions we yearn for peace.

Dear Heart,

Our thoughts are paramount over our heart's feelings. Our notions are supreme and are superior to love. Our minds yearning for control will never end and it will always keep us at war.

Dear Ego,

Whatever thoughts come raging in strife they hold no ground over the influence of the heart's desire. We will always long for belonging and connection to our soul. Love values life and honors our heart's desires because they are our most valued assets.

Dear Heart,

Our beliefs and yearning often clash with what we feel. The conflict between the head and the heart fights one another for different causes. One side desire, one side value.

11

Chapter 11 - A Fight Without a Cause

Dear Ego,

We can live with both desire and value in our life. There does not need to be a fight without a cause. Although our hearts will always fight for love and love always prevails because self-love is a worthy cause.

Dear Heart,

From the beginning of our human life our mind quickly learns we are not worthy. Why fight for love when we already know we are worthless? This seems like a fight without a cause.

Dear Ego,

Our heart breaks when you believe we are worthless. This thought gives us ammunition towards aligning and becoming whole. When we are one, life becomes meaningful and joyful. Humankind depends on our connection to us and with others. Becoming whole and connected within can be achieved without constant state of conflict. With connection our species can die.

CHAPTER 11 - A FIGHT WITHOUT A CAUSE

Dear Heart,

Our conflict exists because the soul wants us to stray from the comfortable and be different. Our ego fights against change, it is fearful of the unknown and being uncomfortable in our own head space.

Dear Ego,

Our spirit just wants us to be authentic, not different. Just be who we are without apologies. Getting uncomfortable in getting to know ourselves is a worthy cause. Becoming whole is noble because becoming our authentic is victory for both sides of us. Authenticity is the end to our nation's divide. Fearing who we are is our death because we never really know ourselves and will always be in a constant state of strife.

Dear Heart,

Authenticity is not accepted in society. People would just not understand who they are because they dread rejection. Therefore, our mind strives to protect our vulnerability and believes showing our softness is a suicide mission.

Dear Ego,

We are not weak if we show vulnerability, it is our strength. It allows us to feel and process our emotions. Vulnerability is a noble cause to believe in.

Dear Heart,

We have been convinced that vulnerability is weakness. We panic at the thought of processing our emotions through being vulnerability and that it is dishonorable.

Dear Ego,

Being open with our feelings takes tenacity but we need our ego to command them and help process what we feel. Please do not overthrow them because we were made to believe vulnerability is weakness. It takes courage to align our heart and our mind.

Dear Heart,

We have been taught to process what we know and what is familiar. Our consciousness lives in the comforts of the known and gets agitated with the uncertainty tries to rule us. Being uncomfortable is uncomfortable and is a foreign state of mind.

Dear Ego,

Our brain is hardwired to seek the familiar, but our love is meant to provide faith when enduring the unknown. Our authenticity is meant to be found in the uncomfortable because that is where evolution is hidden.

Dear Heart,

We will not un-wire without a blow up. Because being in comfort and not exposed is a fight with a cause.

Dear Ego,

Our heart does not want to fight without a cause. Our wisdom knows that fighting ourselves has no purpose. There is no foul in embracing the ego and heart. The only harm done is when we choose not to love ourselves.

Dear Heart,

Life experiences have shaped who we are. Embracing the

heart and not being at battle with it is overwhelming. Our anxiety from life rules keeps us stuck in fear. Fighting to remain in control is all we know and is worthwhile.

Dear Ego,
The antidote to fear is love. Our authenticity is dying to be free, but our mind suppresses it with irrational thoughts. Swallowing fear with love will open us and allow us to be aligned. We lovingly raise our sword in self-defense because we are worthwhile.

Dear Heart,
Ego interjects in strife. Pointing our guns in defense because our limited beliefs are struggling to relinquish control.

Dear Ego,
Thinking we are in control is an illusion and a limited belief. We have many narratives, some true and some lies. Hidden under all the notions is our truth. Sifting through the lies of life can release control and bring us freedom.

Dear Heart,
The power of the mind is its ability to influence. Knowing we are in control is key to the ego's survival. The narratives we believe are our truth.

Dear Ego,
Influencing our authenticity is key to self-love. Having faith in ourselves is survival. The narratives we are told are the passages to finding ourselves.

Dear Heart,

Moving through our thoughts towards our heart causes us fear. That fear creates internal conflict and war within our mind. Our ego wants to protect the narratives and believes the stories are true. Our mind likes to put barricades at the passages to keep us immobile.

Dear Ego,

Our head and our heart are meant to go in different directions. Each side of us is meant to pull the other with force so we can come into alignment. Without the ying and yang balance will never be achieved. Both sides of us are causes to believe in.

Dear Heart,

The game of tug of war between our head and heart has been a part of humans since we existed. The head will tug hard when the heart pulls. The friction between our thoughts and the love in our heart causes rope burn to our soul.

Dear Ego,

Both parts of us pull with force to cause movement towards ourselves. We both need to be certain we are heading towards the right direction in life. The force comes from the internal struggle with or without a cause. Our ego tugs harder to have the mind heard but heart tugs so we can feel our love.

Dear Heart,

This tug of war is tearing us apart

Dear Ego,

CHAPTER 11 - A FIGHT WITHOUT A CAUSE

We can pull together as one towards our heart center for a cause that is worthy.

II

Part 2 - The War Begins

12

Chapter 12 - All War Starts With the Inner Dialog

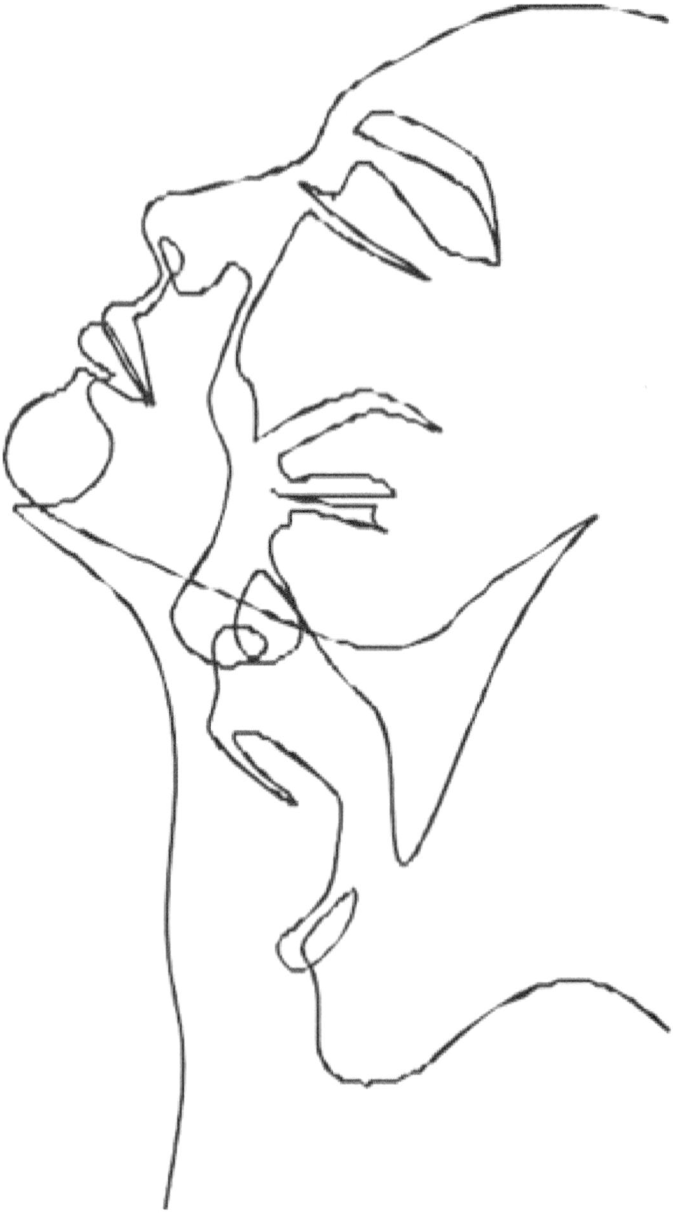

CHAPTER 12 - ALL WAR STARTS WITH THE INNER DIALOG

Dear Heart,

Humans will always drag them self across the center line. The distance of the center line varies from the mind's eye versus the heart center. When it is out of alignment, the inner dialog will fight for a cause and want to be heard. The voice inside is strong, it will wage war against the love in our heart.

Dear Ego,

Our heart can only hear and process our dialog by feeling them. Each thought triggers an emotion inside of us and our love embraces all of them. Love chooses to love not wage war with the mind.

Dear Heart,

The monologue cited is about a civil war. The ego has no space to converse about our feelings and emotions, it only wants our violent and aching thoughts to be validated.

Dear Ego,

It feels like the ego is our enemy. Instead of being at odds with each other, let love be the healer of the hurt of ego. We can replace negative self-talk with loving kindness and positive affirmations. We have the choice to observe our thoughts and process what we feel about them.

Dear Heart,

We often clash, our mind only knows negativity and the heart desires positivity. The chatter in our head is screaming loudly while the heart whispers softly. The inner dialog is always at war.

Dear Ego,

Softness is strength. Our inner most difficult notions are meant to be heard as loving whispers.

Dear Heart

The whispers of the heart are often too quiet for the overwhelming thoughts we think. As we observe the world, our thoughts become skewed and vengeful from what we have seen.

Dear Ego,

Our mind's eye needs to be our eyes, without your observations our heart would never be able to feel emotions. Our heart's voice wants to gently guide the ego's perception to a loving kind dialog with each other to fuel our soul.

Dear Heart,

Our narrative is a violent dialog, it wages war against the loving words in our heart.

13

Chapter 13 - Declaration Of Mind War

Dear Ego,

Any story can be violent enough to start a war, but the narrative can be changed, and new perspectives can be gained without going to war against our heart.

Dear Heart,

Ego rages against change. Its fury declares war against our heart in fear of being forced to change. The peace found within will no longer be because the attack will not be peaceful. Our thoughts are powerful weapons, and they brutally strike at any time. Words of hate are dropped like bombs and blow up our inner world to keep control. The division of self between the head and the heart will always be at the battle front.

Dear Ego,

Our peaceful state will protest the battle, but we will only reciprocate with love. The heart's tactics will fight with love bombs. Ego, kindly consider ceasing fire and ending our internal conflict. Our wholeness will always need each part of us to exist and survive. We need each other to be balanced. We divide for a reason and part of that reason is to come together once again in peace and harmony. Our life will only ever become whole if we learn to coexist together.

Dear Heart,

The gun fire will never cease, the war between us will be a lifelong battle. We are each other's sworn enemies. The inner battle exists all throughout the humans of the world; it is the bloodshed of the mind and heart. It might even be the biggest war in history. Ego is willed and prideful and will fight to the death to concur the heart. We believe the mind's purpose is to defeat the soul.

Dear Ego,

Our heart has been desperately trying to love us unconditionally. It listens intently to the harsh criticism of the ego and knows the lifelong battle very well. Our heart will always fight from a place of love, and it only wants to conquer the harshness within our mind while loving all parts us.

Dear Heart,

We slay love with tanks, war words, and by bombing the love bombs. The slaughter of character allows the great divide between us to exist through our lifetime.

Dear Ego,

This massacre is not necessary. Shooting us down is not the answer. Accepting and loving each part of us is the rebut to end our battle.

CHAPTER 13 - DECLARATION OF MIND WAR

Dear Heart,

We are each other's opposition always. The conflict between us will always exist, it is how we coexist. Mental warfare is our inflicted hunger game. It is in my nature to deprive our heart of soul food and feed our ego to survive.

Dear Ego,

Stop starving us of self-love, we need it to survive. It is neglectful and harmful to deprive our hub of the essentials of life.

Dear Heart,

Neglect is what we were shown through life. The power of the mind builds barricades to protect our vulnerability and wages war against anything that threatens it. Ego's gunfire is imperative for existence without it our ideas and opinions would not exist, putting our biggest asset at risk. Our mind's war is driven to conquer any enemy that it thinks is a threat. The id believes it is superior to the heart because it protects our vulnerability and without our thoughts, we would be mindless with no protection.

Dear Ego,

Our neglect in life was an obstacle meant to be thought about to bring us to the path of self-love and self-care. We are not meant to stay stuck behind the barricade of neglect. In our trenches vulnerability needs the experience of our neglect to give us our freedom from this trauma. It is not meant to bring us war. Our heart will embrace what we think and beliefs about what we endured. We adore our opinions and only want to heal our abusive thoughts, with love. Our journey is meant to endure despair so we can find our love to break the patterns of violent and tormented notions. Our soul wants peace, it does not wish existing in war-torn state.

Dear Heart,
Our peace cannot exist without war first

Dear Ego,
Our heart desires a calm resolution. A treaty to end our devastation? And yes, we know the battle is necessary for our evolution.

Dear Heart
An agreement between us would be easily broken because our intrusive thoughts often arise. They are what we were taught and what we know. Violent thoughts are our certainty, and uncertainty is our fear of love.

Dear Ego,
In fear we are unsafe, and our fear creates our war zone. It paralyses us and keeps us stuck in rivalry. The antidote to fear is love. We need fear to grow and move towards love. It pushes us to the embrace of our heart. Fear and love can exist together in harmony, they do not need a battlefront to continue living independently. We are dependent on each other.

Dear Heart,
We are opposing forces; we need to prepare for battle because we are on the brink of war. Our body is the battlefield that will house our sword fight.

CHAPTER 13 - DECLARATION OF MIND WAR

Dear Ego,

Love has no weapons, only tough love. The heart chooses to love and not wage war. Our soul chooses to be love, to give love and to receive love. This part of us is strong enough to receive any weapon that attacks during battle. Our body may be the battlefield, but our soul is the promised land.

Chapter 14- Rally The Troops

Dear Heart,

The troops know you are defenseless, and the safeguarding thoughts gather like soldiers, ready to attack. Their Amo is self-destruction.

Dear Ego,

Love is the shield that protects us from all battles. Compassion is our protection against the harsh perceptions marching in our mind.

Dear Heart,

Rally your troops and prepare your defenses because the invasion of conception is coming. Dark enemies will invade your heart's space and take your peace. The line of thinking will be intrusive and will demand your attention.

Dear Ego,

The heart will feel the soldiers attacking but our center's

troops will defend our cores space and the soul of our land out of love. Service to us will stand strong in vulnerability and fear will fall.

Dear Heart,

Openness is the heart's weakness and will be easily defeated. Once it is exposed the nuclear force has already caused great harm. Love will be captured in shame.

Dear Ego,

Self-destruction will only cause prolonged suffering. We would fall victim to our own mindset. The hardship would be devastating because the experience of joy, truth and love would be lost in battle.

Dear Heart,

Living in frailness increases the risk of attack. When we are open, we are susceptible to the hurt from the outside world. Our open heart is a boobies trap by wanting to live in a state of joy, truth, and love. Allowing us to be defenseless increases the strength of the ego and size of its troops.

Dear Ego,

Vulnerability is courage. We bare and brave our emotions when we are tender. It allows the mind, body, and soul to be truly seen and heard. Declaring war against the core of who we are will be an uphill battle because our weakness is our resilience.

Dear Heart,

Our emotional warfare will need more than just resilience to withstand our struggle. Our thoughts are very painful, and they fight hard on the battlefield to defend. Our character thrives in our own tragedy of war.

Dear Ego,

Through adversity, is where our resilience evolves. Life's grit thrives from our trauma, and we flourish together in our suffering because persistence only exists when there is a threat against us. Resilience and persistence join forces to conquer fear as one from a place of love.

Dear Heart,

Veteran thoughts are ready to protect our mind's space with combat. Each line of thinking manifests the weapons of words to defeat resilience. With malicious notions we will remain stoic and in our nostalgia our mind stays unchanged. Thinking about change consumes us in fear and from that fear retaliation militia are gathered.

Dear Ego,

Mindset is everything. Imagine life with an open heart and open mind; aligned forces. When in harmony there is no retaliation, only unstoppable empowerment. When the mind embraces the heart instead of fighting against it, we can exist in a sovereign state.

Dear Heart,

Our cynical mindset has kept us divided, like the great wall of China. Our intrusive way of thinking will always try and invade the heart space to devour life's joy with tactical reasoning. Our defensive notions are like a ticking time bomb, ready to explode.

CHAPTER 14- RALLY THE TROOPS

Dear Ego,

Your troops can fight against the heart and our peace, but the heart will heal the hurt with gentle loving kindness. Victory will prevail with kindness to us including our thoughts. If you invade the heart center, it will stand its ground with disaster relief and shift position to force the mind to shift their defenses too.

Dear Heart,

Opposing love from shifting our mindset is our goal in this war. If love persists in our inclination, then our mind will be forced to shift its perspective and alignment is inevitable. Our ego will always resist our alliance.

Dear Ego,

Our life's purpose is to become the best version of us, humans are transient, and we are always shifting. In our hub we need to live in relation to each other, so we can evolve into a better version of ourselves.

Dear Heart,

When the mind shifts into continuity with the heart, there is no purpose. Our life's purpose is then controlled by the embrace of love. We are rallying the troops of tyranny so the ego can remain as the ruler.

Dear Ego,

Our ego is the only part of us that will stand in our way. It keeps us divided but our hub is meant to live life with good will of each other. Mind, body and soul in one body. Our purpose is to coexist in peace not civil war. Our mind is creating sovereignty in our land.

Dear Heart,

The invisible wall within has been rising brick by brick since birth. Each brick stands for a thought, a condition, a label, a rule, a hidden emotion, a system, or a belief. There can be no fear in the mind if it protects itself behind the wall that has been built by the troops defending it.

Dear Ego,

This wall encloses our space, and it creates a closed off space that needs to be an open concept. Being closed off in our world eliminates a life of freedom. To be liberated one needs to be open. Being accessible is how each part of us can connect to ourselves and others. With deep intimacy and softness, the wall can be taken down brick by brick. Our army can stand at ease knowing love is within. Open heart, open mind.

Dear Heart,

We are the mercenary of the wall. The wall of protection is a safeguard from allowing any feelings from invading our head space. It protects us from the weakness of being too soft. The rallied troops always stand guard.

Dear Ego,

The wall is an illusion, it will only shield us from each other. It will stop us from growing closer and prevent us from rising together. One's strength is derived from the relationship they have with them self and that relationship we have within is vital to our survival. Love is not the enemy, nor are the fighting raiders within our head. What is in our head is equally important as to what is in our heart.

Dear Heart,

What is in our head is quite different from what is in our heart. We do not believe there is value in the lines of defense becoming one. Our mind is strong willed and knows oppression very well. Thoughts of self-hatred fuel the war within, and peace is unknown to the territory of the ego. Our character feels stronger when it is in its own head space.

Dear Ego,

With love our heart does not support the battle going on in our head. Our heart wants to be whole and inclusive with the psyche, but we will always love any state of mind or being unconditionally.

Dear Heart,

The defensive troops do not know love and are disconnected from the heart's center. The attack will continue in this mindless world of ours.

Dear Ego,

In strife love vows that we always still show humility and kindness to our broken state of being.

15

Chapter 15 - The Enemies Are Coming Near and Far

Dear Heart,

Warfare it will be, the troops are coming, and they are marching fast. Dark thoughts are like bullets and fear is the atomic bomb. Thoughts of doubt, unworthiness and hate mark our targets and pierce the heart. Bombs are drop and debilitate our soul.

Dear Ego,

The bullets of disheartening beliefs may hit the ticker, but our empathy will heal. The explosion may be self-destructive, but the center will come out stronger from the heaviness of our ashes.

Dear Heart,

The shots fired are meant to cause our heart pain and suffering. The effects from the nuclear explosion are catastrophic and the energy from the blast is meant to destroy our hub here on earth. When we grow as one, the mind is compromised and our selfishness, doubt and insecurity wants to eliminate our evolution.

Dear Ego,
Our troublesome speculation penetrates our heart deeply but the pain from the wound will mend. Our emotions are our defense and will counterattack our intrusive beliefs about ourselves with admiration. Our heart is shielded with light and our light reflects on the darkness so wisdom can be saved.

Dear Heart,
With the capability of near and far enemies the core of us will weaken. Near enemies come in disguise and they tiptoe through the trenches with their guns behind their back. Far enemies trudge through the trenches in camouflage, but they are seen from afar and the target knows they are coming for them.

Dear Ego,
This soul embraces all enemies and will love them unconditionally. With each gloomy outlook that marches closer to the center, the gates will open with a warm welcome. In love the fear created from the loud stomping of marching thoughts will be dissipated.

Dear Heart,
The weight of our disrespect will crush our beat.

Dear Ego,
Our center is strong and can bear the heaviness.

Dear Heart,

Our hesitation tally together like heavy and powerful army tanks, ready to fire as front-line defense. The fire power from a tank is powerful and destructive. The mind's armor is ready to protect our reflections.

Dear Ego,

Any tank is just a hub. It may shoot raging debates like wildfire, but tanks are still a grounded defense.

Dear Heart,

A tank with grounded mobility is free to shoot thoughts at any time. Bullets, rockets, or missiles are all catastrophic once released.

Dear Ego,

Our heart is armored to embrace the pain from injuries of the shots fired. Holding space for our defensive behavior is how our love can open the top of the tank to let the light in.

Dear Heart,

The mind is like a ticking time bomb and each doubtful thought is closer to an explosion.

Dear Ego,

With rupture comes repair. With repair comes healing, with healing comes understanding. With understanding comes acceptance. None of this evolution is possible without the bomb. Each time we explode we learn to become closer to our core.

Dear Heart,

How many shots to the heart can we take before it breaks? Our ID tosses out shame, guilt, and fear like grenades.

Dear Ego,

Love does not fear the war within, and our compassion is not afraid of any weapon. When our mind fears, we love. When guilty we find pride in ourselves. If shame finds us, dignity lies below the surface. Every grenade thrown is a pathway to our heart.

Dear Heart,

Ego thrives in coercion. Terrorizing our emotions with bombs, grenades and guns is part of our spitefulness.

Dear Ego,

These attacks against us are sins to ourselves. But they also hold value in finding our values.

Dear Heart,

The ego's intention is to target the heart. Sometimes our army attacks hard while other times the deploy misses the target.

Dear Ego,

Intentionally wanting to destroy one's spirit is deceiving only if the target is unaware. The heart will find self-respect in deceit and create self-love from the harm to find mercy and truth. Once the heart is aware our army can stand strong in unity because we are then one.

Dear Heart,

The troops have rallied together among our thoughts. Devastating thoughts will win this war and the ego will prevail. Our mind is filled with unaware veterans with years of social conditioning. They stand strong in their beliefs and remain stuck in nostalgia. They only know suffering and they will defend suffering's honor to protect it.

Dear Ego,

Keep faith, even the oldest thought can be set free from our conditioning. By letting go of the past, thoughts can help heal oneself. In letting go we can release our pain. The soldiers of negativity can change their belief system and mindset as they march closer to the heart center.

Dear Heart,

The enemies march towards the center to conquer it with fear with thoughts of unworthiness, guilt, and shame.

Dear Ego,

Conquering our heart space will not be easy. Our loving heart space will be defended with words of affirmation, kindness, and self-love. The light within wants to shine bright to lead the way for the knights of darkness.

Dear Heart,

The power struggle between the heart and ego is real. Your defenseless veterans are less than prepared for the fighting sentiments from the ego.

Dear Ego,

There should be no inequality within us. We are both equal and we both need to be whole. Our heart is not greater than our mind and our mind is not more than our heart. Our thought patterns limit and restrict our co-existence and equilibrium.

Dear Heart,

The intellectual army is the opposing force to equality. Our beliefs will hinder a change of heart, and they want to stay static. Trying to influence our views will not create a calm state of mind. Nor will it create balance between our head and our heart.

Dear Ego,

To create equality in our existence is not just about changing your mind, it is about aligning our forces to be centered in unity, so we are in a calm state of being.

Dear Heart,

Armour your heart because the command of the head is going to knock us out of alignment. Our scrutiny will break our heart. The intent to shatter it into a million pieces so it cannot be whole again.

Dear Ego,

The space within is expansive and limitless even when broken. It has the ability to embrace any intrusive company that tries to invade this place. The affection within this kingdom will show up with open arms for indifference of the armed forces.

16

Chapter 16 - The Battlefield

Dear Heart,

Our troops have prepared for battle and are ready to invade the expansive space where the kingdom lies. Our soldiers are made up of all types; seals, marine corps and green berets all trained to be ruthless in combat. Each ready to use negativity as their weapons.

Dear Ego,

Our heart does not fear the soldiers or the weapons they use. They will be embraced with loving arms.

Dear Heart,

Attacking thoughts will sweep through the psyche like automatic gun fire and bombs dropping. Shots through the heart and explosives detonated to blow up our world. We will feel the toxicity like chemical warfare.

Dear Ego,

CHAPTER 16 - THE BATTLEFIELD

Our heart is shielded with love, the aftermath of an explosion will only bring hope. Toxicity is already all around us and humankind still prevails. Love will never fear the weapons that cause our suffering because our core knows that a fight response is needed for evolution.

Dear Heart,
Internalizing life's grenades thrown at us is second nature to the mind. Automatically we inhale the toxicity from the gases produced from war.

Dear Ego,
Fumes are toxic, weapons cause physical pain and enemies cause mental suffering. We are surrounded by the hurt of the world, and we are conditioned to internalize the battle, even if it is not our battle. The battlefield between the head and the heart is needed to have peace.

Dear Heart,
Creating pain to generate prolonged suffering is the mind's determined march to the battlefield.

Dear Ego,
Trauma leads us into many battles and enemy conflict will always invade our head space. The heart and mind are always at war but our love for ourselves will always defend us from the weapons of pain used against us.

Dear Heart,
Defense is warranted but the mind has a lot of war strategies. Eventually the weapons used will injury our soul with thoughts

of shame and guilt. Feelings of isolation will destroy the heart's center.

Dear Ego,

One's soul can be shaken to the core, but it will always exist. Even if we are burnt to the ground in battle, we will always rise strong from the ashes.

Dear Heart,

When our thoughts scorch us, we get scared. The scars left are grotesque. When burnt we are left for dead. Our fiery beliefs make us believe we are unworthy because of our disfigurement.

Dear Ego,

We are always worthy of ourselves in any body. Scars heal with new tissue. In the regrowth it will look different. If one embraces the new self, they can heal and evolve from their war wounds.

Dear Heart,

The enemies are near and afar. They trek forward in anger with their swords drawn, ready to slice and pierce all parts of us. They fill our space with contempt.

Dear Ego,

On the battlefield, we will honor apathy with empathy.

Dear Heart,

Empathy will fuel the soldier's psyche with disgust.

Dear Ego,

CHAPTER 16 - THE BATTLEFIELD

When disgust arrives, we will trust it and embrace it. We will sit with it and hold space for it. Disgust will not destroy us because deep down we know all parts of us are beautiful.

Dear Heart,

Our pride will not allow the heart warm welcome of trust. The shame within us is also deep and keeps the beautiful parts of us hidden.

Dear Ego,

All parts of the war within have elegance even the negative emotions, we just need to cut the shame around the emotions so we can see the grace within.

Dear Heart,

Shame lives in our world and in the space of ego. Our humiliation and our entire being will lack peace from the distress created by our egotism.

Dear Ego,

Peace can only triumph from the dark experiences we journey through on the battlefield. Trekking the war of the mind and heart will bring darkness and light, hardness, and softness. Although, it would not be a true battle without fear and love.

Dear Heart,

Our mind is the dark knight casting shadows of doubt across the land.

Dear Ego,

Our heart is the white knight bringing conviction to our mind and peace within.

Dear Heart,
Trying to defeat the opinion of the mind with the beliefs of the heart will be daunting. Our thought's resistance is powerful enough to debilitate us into despair.

Dear Ego,
The influence of hope and the gift of faith relieves despair.

Dear Heart,
In this war zone, words of war begin the battle. We are not enough. We are not strong enough, we are not beautiful enough, we are not smart enough, we are not rich enough, we are not good enough.

Dear Ego,
On the heart's battle line, we are enough, in everything that we do.

Dear Heart,
On the minds front we are stupid, incapable, worthless, helpless, and disgusting.

Dear Ego,
Within the lines of love, we are brilliant, capable, worthy, strong and beautiful.

17

Chapter 17 - Fighting For Our Deadly Sins

Dear Heart,

We are also prideful, greedy, wrathful, envious, lustful, glutenous. and slothful. We live in sin and have betrayed our heart with many deadly sins. Our mind believes the story that this is who we are. Its wounds are rooted deeply.

Dear Ego,

Pride can be sinister, but it can also be beautiful. Sometimes it gives us the satisfaction we need to survive. It is confidence and self-respect, and feelings of confidence and self-love are not sinful. It is when we are too prideful, we devalue us or others. Devaluing any human spirit, including our own, causes destruction, when the purpose of pride is to generate self-awareness and love.

Dear Heart,

The fight within convinces us of our conceit and arrogance.

This part of our mind thrives on being self-centered. It is the source of our ego and keeps the mind stuck in a constant state of fight response.

Dear Ego,

Being too prideful is not self-love, it is just shyness of self-hatred. Not letting go of our pride can really cause a lot of harm. Living in contempt is suppressing because it suppresses our authenticity. Simply, because we think we are better than others and we believe our authentic self is not enough.

Dear Heart,

Self-destruction combat is the ego's comfort zone. Being cozy in the destruction zone keeps the mind at peace and segregated from the heart.

Dear Ego,

One does not need to live in a fight, flight or freeze war zone. We can have peace by trying to become whole and not staying segregated. Becoming whole is very comforting to our whole self. We deny ourselves happiness when we live in destruction and distant from our heart center. Not seeking inner peace is extremely selfish.

Dear Heart,

It is human nature to be greedy and selfish, it is what we know. Our mind wants what it wants when it wants it. Our society has created a self-obsessed population of material objects, money, and power. We feel powerful and in control when we achieve material objects and forget what the heart needs.

CHAPTER 17 - FIGHTING FOR OUR DEADLY SINS

Dear Ego,

Instant gratification is just brief rushes of joy that instantly slip away. It is not sustainable. Once gone, the mind feels empty again and is ready to fight again because it is trying to find happiness from a material source to fuel its greed. If one can see the beauty of the mundane and gratitude, then a constant state of bliss can be kept. One of our life's purposes is to learn to validate the intangible items from our heart, instead of trying to satisfy our ego with tangible items.

Dear Heart,

Our ego processes and fights for what the outside world has taught us. It resonates with the filth that feeds our mind. The ego does not have the ability to connect with the joy found in trivial things.

Dear Ego,

We always could connect with ourselves instead of fighting with ourselves.

Dear Heart,

Our wrath from a life of trauma, neglect and isolation prevents us from connecting with anything. Anger fuels the war we have imposed on ourselves.

Dear Ego,

Anger is an intense feeling but can be released with good humor and kindness towards us. It does not need to be fuel that starts the fire within, it can be the feeling that opens the pathway to kindness.

Dear Heart,

Our mind lusts for kindness from others. When it is not received, we become hostile ready for combat against anyone who has denied our desire.

Dear Ego,

Kindness is something we can give to ourselves and others. It is within us, and we must learn to know that we are worthy of kindness. Once we give it to ourselves, we do not need to fight life desiring it.

Dear Heart,

We are always jealous of people who can give kindness to others and themselves. We envy their humility.

Dear Ego,

Humility is intangible and is a worthy trait to aide in connection with us. Instead of pushing it away in fear of it be open to it.

Dear Heart,

Fighting off our humility is the self-center focus of our egotism. We want to keep in control of who we portray to the world.

Dear Ego,

Swallow your pride and learn love for yourself. The inappropriate desire to keep control is an overindulgence of power. Instead of having strife for control, fight for self-empowerment.

CHAPTER 17 - FIGHTING FOR OUR DEADLY SINS

Dear Heart,

Our ego is very reluctant to make any effort to self-empower ourselves. This mind believes destruction is empowerment.

Dear Ego,

Laziness in self-evolution is the equivalent to shattering of the heart.

Dear Heart,

If we are still broken, the ego's declaration of war is over because the mind stays in power. If the rain of control is the throne through sloth, then this war was a victory.

Dear Ego,

The cardinal sins we impose on ourselves do not define us; they are only part of us. Our heart will embrace all sin and ask for forgiveness. Our authenticity will see the good and the lessons from the sinister parts of us. Our love embraces all parts of us because it knows they have something to teach us. Each part of that is shattered will mend back together through compassion.

18

Chapter 18 - Enduring The War

Dear Heart,

Our sin gives a pathway to the ego to keep us in shame. Our sinister parts give strength to the troops rallying in the mind. The negative marching soldiers are our pillar to endure the war. The guilt of our past keeps us suffering.

Dear Ego,

We endure suffering so we can find freedom. Endurance cannot exist without suffering because it is our will to survive. We experience unnecessary suffering when we starve ourselves from love during our battles, but our faith will grant us the endurance we need to survive the fight. The hardship of life fuels our soul with the strength we need to move through pain and become the highest version of ourselves.

Dear Heart,

Hidden deep within the bunkers are our burdens of heavy thoughts. Enduring these gloomy depriving thoughts with only faith may prove challenging. Shifting one's mindset is a daunting task because we are hardwired to believe the worst about ourselves. Our ego thrives on these conditions and combative ideas generate in the bunker we are stuck in. Believing self-love will prevail over years of war in our mind seems impossible to reach.

Dear Ego,

Our soul's purpose is to evolve into the highest version of ourselves through self-love. We are meant to endure adversity, so that we can feel the pain and heal it with love. Through tribulations lessons are found. In these teachings we learn to undo what we learnt. We get to break patterns taught, we get to deprogram and rewire how we want. Without enduring the pain, one will never really feel the abundance of love given during our time to heal.

We need to lose faith, to find faith. When faith is restored during a civil war it is stronger than ever, like the phoenix rising from its ashes. Our heart is meant to endure all of it.

Dear Heart,

Ego is the true test to our ability to self-preserve. Through all our journeys into darkness the violence in our mind is the real testament to the endurance of the heart.

Dear Ego,

All violence of war causes deep injury and hurt in our heart, but it is necessary for steadfastness. Our unwavering unconscious self-admiration embraces all pain to endure and persevere.

19

Chapter 19 - The Wall of Protection

Dear Heart,

If the heart is willing to endure the war, then a pivot in war strategy is vital to this victory. If we cannot invade our center's space, we will build a wall so tenderness cannot breach the mastermind.

Dear Ego,

Your army is strong, and it has built the tallest walls out of the toughest materials. Nothing and no one can get through.

Ego, you are the mace that breaks the heart.

You are the only one who can disguise as a friend only to be let in right through the portcullis.

You are the foe that has struck around the shield using a flail.

You are the enemy that emotionally attacks us beyond the walls that you built.

Dear Heart,

In our stupidity love has been deceived by your enemy. If we

CHAPTER 19 - THE WALL OF PROTECTION

were smarter, we would look for the malicious climbing over the wall disguised as a foe. Once the opposition has been spotted, counterattack and play their game war. Why would our heart let them in? They may serve us but on the war path they will try and rob us of our truth, so it is never heard.

Dear Ego,

Stupidity is not allowing our enemies to enter because in our loving state we embrace all. Any thoughts or feelings that climb over the wall and march towards the center need to be seized, not released. We only see invaders as loved ones, never a foe. We observe them to feel and receive the lesson from a place of love. Anything that comes over the wall will serve our entirety and bring truth to our life.

Dear Heart,

The barrier has been built to keep the truth hidden. Built to segregate our thoughts from our heart. Within the framework we can keep our deliberation stuck behind the facade.

Dear Ego,

Apprehension might be stuck behind the structure, but it is invisible to our heart because it still feels disrespectful and detrimental beliefs towards ourselves. Pessimism towards ourselves is always felt at our core.

Dear Heart,

The brick and mortar of the mind's beliefs is the physical safe space where we think we are disgusting, worthless and not enough. It is a place of comfort.

Dear Ego,

The bricks are strong and reinforced with self-hatred, but self-love can climb over anything, and light can seep into any cracks.

Dear Heart,

Self-love will cause the wall to collapse

Dear Ego,

When the walls crumble, then there will be a collapse in the state of mind. The mind will lose control, and it is forced to let go of the hurdles holding us back from our authenticity.

Dear Heart,

But our head space is the part of us that holds fear. Letting the walls fall to let go of the fear is why we build the structure in the first place. It wants to barricade our understanding and keep us living in a place of terror.

Dear Ego,

Why live behind the walls in uneasiness when we could exist in love with no divider. Please give yourself permission to break down the obstacles. Because the obstacle is you.

Dear Heart,

Our proximity is not meant to be close; the barricade is meant to keep us distant.

Dear Ego,

We are meant to be whole as one state of being. Not divided instead; mind, body, and soul. Our closeness cannot be sepa-

CHAPTER 19 - THE WALL OF PROTECTION

rated by the bricks. The great wall is just an illusion, love will always find a way over, around or through any hurdle. Our heart will find a way to triumph pass any obstacle.

Dear Heart,

State of mind keeps the structure high and the mortar airtight. To triumph the heart soldiers might be climbing the wall forever to invade the mind's space.

Chapter 20 - The Inner War

Dear Ego,

We all need to climb and fall; this is how we conquer the peak and rise to the best version of ourselves. We are brave enough to hike to any height.

Dear Heart,

The inner war between the head and the heart has deep roots. It started the day we were born and the civil war within grows in the way we were raised. Our beliefs and values bestowed upon us shape our mind. What we are taught to believe develops a sickened head space and the dark values cast shadow over our hearts. Our traumas in life are like boobies traps, one trigger they explode.

Dear Ego,

The inner war starts with the mind falling victim to a false belief system. The mind is so powerful it can cultivate many thoughts like a cult of troops ready to fight for all the distorted values of someone else's opinion. Only a Mind shift from a core shift can change our mindset, the shift in both parts of us can be the salvation of this war.

Dear Heart

Our inner conflict is like a sea of blood. Our guilt and shame are our bloodshed, and our unworthiness is the bloodbath from the heaviness of thinking we are not enough.

Dear Ego,

Shift towards the heart center to feel peace from the anguish of the bloodshed. Release control of the swinging sword to feel relief from the cuts. Go inward to mend the wounds of the bloodbath. Within the heart space there is security and infinite mending. The healing space within will cover us and keep us safe like a bomb shelter. Within the close quarters worth and love are found.

Dear Heart,

Our mind yearns for peace, but our ego is very tactile and does want to succumb to victory of the heart. It keeps us convinced that peace is unattainable, and we need to wage war. Our culture desire worth but ego cultivates a mentality that having worth is a hopeless cause because we will always be worthless. Our thought patterns allow the battle to survive.

Dear Ego,

Patterns are powerful but they can be broken with sheer will power cultivated from the desire to change them. The self-love we desire will always fight to prevail over our ego.

Dear Heart,

Our mind only knows patterns, and our feelings and emotions about our ingrained patterns create strife in our head space. We fear what we feel, and we do not know how to rationalize them. Ego fights against our powerful emotions and wages war towards the heart to keep our thoughts safe in what it knows. Our egotism cannot let go of the control it thinks it has.

Dear Ego,

We only ever live in love or fear. Fear is what creates war in any space. Know our heart space is joy, truth, and love. Within the energy of our soul this is no fight, only peace in any dilemma.

Dear Heart,

Our dilemma will always oppose the tranquility of the heart.

Dear Ego,

There does not have to be a dilemma, we could have a truce between us. Our truce would eliminate our conflicts and move us closer to each part of ourselves. Aligning the mind and heart can be the catalyst to ending the inner war. Conflicting beliefs would diminish if we were to align, and we would become whole.

Dear Heart,

We are separate entities. Mind versus heart. Sometimes we think our soul does not exist. Being separate entities makes us each other's competition and we will always have an inner struggle.

Dear Ego,

Our soul is our life source and the essence of who we are. It wants to embrace our beautiful mind and our loving heart. The soul's purpose is meant to bring us together to live in harmony. Within is where our light is found, and it will shed light on our darkness.

Dear Heart,
If our soul really exists then why hasn't it broken through the mortar of our wall, to stop the inner conflicts?

Dear Ego,
Beloved ego, it has, many times. Our light seeps through all the cracks in our wall during our darkest hours, giving us comfort in despair. The glimpse of light we feel during our suffering is our salvation. At that moment it feels like peace and the internal war has stopped.

Dear Heart,
Why can't our peaceful moments be kept? Why do we repeatedly always return to suffering over and over?

Dear Ego,
Dear one, because we know no difference. Our patterns and conditioning have only shown us what the world wants us to be. But our heart knows us differently and wants to show the ego what unconditional love is. Our soul desires us to experience life together from a place of light. This is why we feel the rays of light in our darkness. It is trying to bring us to the right state of mind to show us our authenticity. It desperately wants to break through the wall of society and show you who you really are. Only our mind can be the part of us to let go of what it knows and bring break our barriers to find our abundant self.

Dear Heart,

Our life is a preconditioned existence, we are taught guilt and shame from the outside world from the time we enter it. How can our mind break through years of social conditioning and stop our internal conflict of what we think versus what we know?

Dear Ego,

Many people in our world are sleeping and they never awake to the world that exists within them. Our life's purpose is to become the best version of ourselves and shift our mindset to believe in keeping faith with the knowing that everything we need comes from within. Outside influences do not hinder us, we hinder ourselves. We listen to the world around us and believe what they tell us, instead of listening to what is in our heart. Alliance between the head and the heart will be the breakthrough of our own existence. Keeping faith in ourselves will lead us to our truth and detach us from the illusion of what the world tells us is true.

Dear Heart,

Our ego sometimes wants to remain sleeping, it is why it fights to survive in a war-torn reality. It values the glory of staying asleep and living in what it knows. It wages war against change and growth because it is resistant to a mind shift. What we have been taught to believe hinders the heart, but not the mind. Coming to an alliance with our heart seems like a difficult process. The soldiers that march on in our mind enjoy the illusion of our war and they do not want to let go of the illusion because they are afraid.

CHAPTER 20 - THE INNER WAR

Dear Ego,

In darkness one sleeps, in light we awake. There is glory for both parts of us to live life whole. Even living in uncertainty can be joyful because in those moments the unexpected can arise. Life in the unknown is magical and full of opportunities but only if we have an open mind.

Dear Heart,

Our ID is full of expectations. Inner war exists because we believe that our life should look and be a certain way. Our mind has been trained to be close minded like soldiers training for combat. It is like outside influences trained us for an unnecessary conflict within ourselves. Has the world been lying to us?

Dear Ego,

My loved one, the world does not know any better, most of humanity is unaware of their truth. If this is what they believe to be true, then the world is not lying to us. But we know better in our heart, and we are lying to ourselves. Before one awakes, it is an illusion of what life is supposed to be. The illusion is meant to give us the path to our truth. Only we can be the one to look within and find the meaning of our life. Know life can be what we want it to be and within our home is joy, truth, and love not war.

Dear Heart,

Our ego does not know better, it wants to remain sleeping with the rest of the world so it can think it is safe. Lying to ourselves is easier than being honest with ourselves. In our mind the illusion is real and remains real in the light of everyone else.

Our beliefs tell us that there is certainty in placating to what we are supposed to be in our life.

Dear Ego,

Trusting the uncertainty in who you will become only happens by taking a leap of faith to trust your heart instead of external voices of misled world. Outside voices have invaded your thoughts and created the clash within.

Dear Heart,

Taking the risk to target and shoot at our thought processes is very unsettling. The marching men in our mind clasp to certainty. Our soldiers fear the unknown and they are trained to fight for a cause which are the certainties of life.

Dear Ego,

Nothing is certain in life. Maintaining inner conflict and holding our love hostage is not the answer for security in life.

Dear Heart,

Being safe in our mind's space is the design of the ego. There is no room to welcome the heart's space with open arms. Our security is found in the beliefs we know. Our wits will always want inner war to keep our beliefs guarded.

21

Chapter 21

Chapter 21 – A Vulnerable Attack

Dear Ego,

Our heart's center is the most vulnerable part of us. Its softness is like the dust particles landing peacefully on the war zone after the dust settles from the war waged. Its tenderness will heal the wounds from the gunshots fired. Its security is unconditional love in any state of being.

Dear Heart,

On the battlefield our social conditioning fights our vulnerability with jabbing words of malice. Landmines are full of unworthiness, shame, and guilt. Jousting the heart's trust and faith is the mission of our troops.

Dear Ego,

Daily battles against our vulnerability are unnecessary. Vulnerability is the core of us and cannot be won in any war. Attacking our predisposition with our mind can be catastrophic in the moment but it is not despair because the heart knows this too shall pass. The heart's strength can heal all war wounds and find courage to love us once again through any adversity.

Dear Heart,

Our ego defends the power of the mind because vulnerability is our weakness. Living in vulnerability only puts us at risk of being hurt.

Dear Ego,

Everything in life is a risk because nothing is permanent, and everything can hurt us. Everything is transient and ends. It is painful when it ends but the endings being openings that allows us to accept the outcome. Our self-trust flourishes when our mind takes the chance to embrace our defenselessness instead of defending against it.

Dear Heart,

When we are vulnerable, we are exposed and defenseless. Attacking it seems like an effortless victory.

Dear Ego,

Our heart is not the enemy to be victorious over and an attack against our vulnerability will not be easy. Even if the ego conquers the heart, love will always be a part of us and can never be lost, only gained.

Dear Heart,

Exploiting us will be a vulnerable attack to the heart. We are flawed by design and the psyche likes to beat on those flaws.

CHAPTER 21

Dear Ego,

Our fondness for ourselves will counterattack the vulnerable attack. It will thrive in self-intimacy with all parts of us that are exposed.

Dear Heart,

That is what the ID fears exposing who we are.

Dear Ego.

Showing our softness to the world is a noble cause because our authenticity is a cause worth fighting for.

Dear Heart,

Our mind cannot handle it if we show the world who we are and we are not loved or accepted. This is why our ego attacks our heart's vulnerability to protect it from rejection.

22

Chapter 22 - Waging War Out of Love or Die in Fear

Dear Ego,

We only live in love or fear. So, one can fight for love, or they can die in fear.

Dear Heart,

Our intelligence perceives everything as a threat and our thoughts wage war in fear. We only have the mental ability to live in fight mode, flight mode, or freeze mode.

Dear Ego,

Sometimes threats are real and sometimes they are just perceived threats. Waging love towards any of those threats can help learn how to discern them. Then we can rationalize the risk from them.

Dear Heart,

Our psyche loves to live in fear waged by our emotions. Sometimes the emotions are too overwhelming; the self-centered succumbs to fear and wants to give up.

Dear Ego,
The core of us wants to battle fear with love. It knows the only way through despair is with heart and soul.

Dear Heart,
Being overwhelmed by despair is the greatest power of reasoning because we can then believe all hope is lost. Without hope there is only fear, and the ego can keep thriving.

Dear Ego,
Emotions of desperation and anguish caused by despair can only be fought with one antidote, love. Our heart will wage war to support self-love by using the power of love to concur our darkest thoughts.

Dear Heart,
Self-love is uncomfortable, and fear is nestled cozy in our bunker. When our psyche senses emotions of love it automatically perceives it as a threat and fears the uncertainty of love. Instantly from fear we wage war against it.

Dear Ego,
When fear dominates us, show affection towards the nerves. Love will wage war with fear, ironically not to be victorious over fear but to embrace it. We need both emotions to survive. We can live with both love and fear, duality.

Dear Heart,

How can one live in love or fear? Believing that duality is achievable seems like a difficult concept.

Dear Ego,

Our heart is love and our ego is fear but we both exist within ourselves. Learning to acknowledge both emotions is crucial to our world's survival. We are one and are meant to be aligned and coexist within ourselves. Knowing and embracing both parts of our world would end the inner. Trusting who we are, and the process can bring us peace in our mind and our heart. Duality exist within us; they are just equal parts of us to us and are us.

Dear Heart,

Our reasoning only seems to be to be acquitted with strife and usually rejects love to remain detached. Trusting the process of becoming whole is hard. Keeping war waging is much easier.

Dear Ego,

Being detached from one part of us means you do not have any trust in our authentic self. Living in fear of who we are is cruel to our soul's growth. Self-love is our preservation to trusting the inner battle to our authenticity.

Dear Heart,

Detachment in the mind is connected to anything or anyone, including ourselves. Depriving us from love is security to the ego. Self-love is untrustworthy to our deep innermost thoughts.

23

Chapter 23 - Trusting The Battle

Dear Ego,

One needs to trust the battle and our heart center keeps faith that the battle is for good reason. Love is built on trust and trusting in ourselves during our inner war. Believe it will always keep us safe during our inner conflict and faith that our life struggles unfold as they should. They are meant to be trusted for the life lesson they will give us if we believe in it.

Dear Heart,

Our thoughts are hard to trust because they are impure. It is hard to know that everything we go through is part of the process. It is even more difficult to learn the lesson of discernment. Discerning ourselves and other parts in the process seems like the most daunting part of the process.

Dear Ego,

Listening to our heart is a big part of the process that is often ignored. Trusting in our intuition is often neglected like the barracks on the battlefield. Believing in our good and fighting for love against our dark forces that exist within is part of our journey that we need to learn trust. Know with conviction the purity of the heart and trust in the difficulty of the process to bring us to our purest form.

Dear Heart,

We know that our belief system will always try to lead our heart away from its purity. The insecurity of the mind struggles with the battle. Egotism will lead us down the easy road to the preconceived notion of what we think is true. Our ego will try and convince us that there is nothing safe in our world or our own skin.

Dear Ego,

Our trusting heart will never fall victim to not being safe because our core knows we are safe within our own skin. We have faith in our life's battles forced in front of our heart because our heart trusts it is the way to our freedom. Our heart embraces the fight we are faced with because we know deep within it will be our evolution.

Dear Heart,

Our belief system is to trust no one, including ourselves. We strongly believe we need to attack our trust within ourselves and others, so our discernment is dismantled to disable the trajectory we are supposed to go.

Dear Ego,

To become wholehearted, we need to accept that all parts of our journey are meant to be part of our life. When we accept this, we can accept who we really are. Embracing all parts of ourselves and trusting in all life's hardships on our voyage is the treaty that will make us whole.

Dear Heart,
Learning to feel whole in who we are is a lost cause because self-doubt will always cast shadow on our authenticity and generates a lack of confidence within our own process. Our mind consistently compartmentalized everything to keep us segregated from being whole and it creates doubt within.

Dear Ego,
The battle we have in our mind is not trustworthy to our soul. It has tormented our core and has delayed the end of our war significantly. When we consistently fight with ourselves our freedom is lost to the darkest parts of our mind.

Dear Heart,
Freedom is not meant to be easy, and trust is earned. Our mind will always try to oppress our heart's freedom, and our ego will always be uneasy about trusting ourselves. Our subconscious will continuously want to slaughter faith and keep skepticism strong.

Dear Ego,
The absence of coercion is our individual right. Our heart will always value our freedom and live in a place of openness and free will. Free from the fight in our mind our consciousness will strive to trust our whole heartiness and will always believe in our process.

Dear Heart,

Betraying ourselves is the prerogative of the ego. Trust ceases to exist in our war-torn world of unbroken promises.

Dear Ego,

Regaining faith and being vulnerable during the process is part of our healing journey. We need to lose our whole self on life's journey to find our way home. Self-evolution can only improve with impaired and broken trust. Giving one space to repair our rupture from ourselves is an integral part of rebuilding our trust in who we are. Forgiveness of our mistakes is ownership of our vulnerable states, but awareness of our feelings is key to change and the desire to come home to ourselves.

III

PART 3 - Ending The War and The Aftermath

24

Chapter 24 - Impose Gratitude on Thy Enemy

Dear Heart,

Mistrust in our vulnerability is our uncertainty and our battle against our authenticity. Our ego is unknowing of the love within and therefore unappreciative of self-love. We know our heart's tenderness to love but our ego is hardened to the notion of love. Often our mind gives up on knowing the softness of love.

Dear Ego,

If we cannot impose gratitude for the love we have within, we will only ever be our own worst enemy and we will only ever know the pain of the shots fired against us.

Dear Heart,

Pain is the Ego's guilty pleasure. Gratitude will dissolve our pain and weaken who we are.

Dear Ego,

Both pain and pleasure are required for us to exist in balance. Our heart will always accept pain and pleasure as a learning opportunity. Love will be kind to our suffering and surrender to our joy. Gratitude to the enemy of pain is our openness to growth. Gratitude to the pleasures of the heart is our continuous expansion in life.

Dear Heart,

The troops in our mind perceive pleasure as the enemy and believe pain is our mentor and alley.

Dear Ego,

Our heart comforts our agony like it is our greatest leader. Gratitude for the suffering imposed during war is our favorite soldier in life. When we are antagonistic, we stand strong against the torture that we impose in our mind. Our soul knows we cannot have real joy without the slaughter of ourselves caused by our own self demise.

Dear Heart,

The unconscious parts of us do not resonate with pleasure because it only exists in pain. Our mindset does not have a lot of flexibility and stagnates listening to our heart. The power struggle of trusting our heart and only observing our biased thoughts is real. We judge our hearts and trust our misconceptions. Being thankful for the heart's longing is not a concept in our mind.

Dear Ego,

Gratitude is the gateway to openness of the mind, body, and

soul. Being thankful for the hardened parts of ourselves can shift our mindset and open our heart center. A change of heart can open our mind to new perspectives. Francis Bacon once said, "Knowledge is power." Our heart can embrace power while our mind knows power as one, instead of fighting over us to maintain the separation of self.

Dear Heart,
   We honestly think there is no gratification in our thoughts of knowing the value of our heart's feelings.

Dear Ego,
   Love is grateful for the ego and understands the value of it. Our love can help the ego rationalize our truth. In the deepest part of our heart, we desire devotion from our ego to develop our authenticity. We give thanks to the enemies of the mind when they agree to put their guard down to embrace who we are meant to be.

Dear Heart,
   How can one be thankful for despair created in our mind?

Dear Ego,
   Because despair brings us closer to faith. Self-growth and self-love needed to experience suffering to receive the gift of gratitude. It allows us to keep faith in knowing everything will be okay

Dear Heart,
   The ego will always choose fear over faith because our mind is afraid to expand, and we are comforted by our pain. The mind's

battle will want to stay stuck in the suffering we know.

Dear Ego,

Without gratitude we only know suffering. Both suffering and gratitude serve a purpose in our life, and we need both to survive and evolve. Remain open minded to faith. Choosing faith over fear is the catalyst to believing in oneself. Despair only leads us astray from the heart for a fleeting period but eventually we find our way back through the darkness into the light from our faith.

Dear Heart,

Despair can destroy us. It can put an end to our existence in a moment's notice.

Dear Ego,

Finding gratitude for the lessons from the hurt will lead us to a place of love. Which will save us in all difficult moments.

25

Chapter 25 - Despair in a World of War

Dear Heart,

Our world is at war. One part of us thinks we are living in despair and the other part of us feels love all at the same time. The enemy only wants the destruction of our worth that we built. Wholeness and love are hidden in the wounds of war so the violence against our humanity can stay still exist.

Dear Ego,

Abusing ourselves so the psyche will still exist if love were to prevail is not a tactical response. Questioning, "will this part of

CHAPTER 25 - DESPAIR IN A WORLD OF WAR

me still survive the war if love is victorious is more rational.

Dear Heart,

Our psyche believes certain parts of us will no longer exist and that self-destruction will be overthrown. This shift and revolution may cause our minds' world to end and despair to crumble.

Dear Ego,

Not a revolution but an evolution. Not destruction but self-growth as one. We would diversify through our light and darkness. Moments of despair will still exist, but our love will heal it and guide us through any shadowing times.

Dear Heart,

The ego is blinded by the light within and feels more in control and powerful within our gloom. The thought of replacing dimness with illumination is a change difficult to acknowledge. The absence of light keeps us in despair in this world of war.

Dear Ego,

The purpose of light is not to remove the darkness. Its purpose is to flicker in the absence of light to help guide us through our dimness. Light is our life source but cannot exist if it has nothing to illuminate.

Dear Heart,

If we put an end to our suffering while in despair, neither light nor darkness will exist.

Dear Ego,

In our world of self-destruction, we are reborn every day. Our heart and soul desire to be revived as one: mind, body, and soul. Living our life being rather than a state of being.

Dear Heart,

Our ego wants to remain unconscious. Despair is the true test of our testament to our existence. In the loss of hope our life may end

Dear Ego,

Within any state of destruction, our worries give us purpose, our sorrow gives us joy, and despair is hope. Duality exists all around us and within us, it is passage to existence, not the end of our life.

Dear Heart,

If we are duality, how can we ever be one? Why try to become whole if we can never truly exist without each part of ourselves?

Dear Ego,

Dualism will always be a part of our world, only through acceptance of both sides of us do we become whole.

Dear Heart,

Acknowledging our feelings and allowing them to pass does not come easy to our mind to accommodate. We strike against ourselves, so we do not allow ourselves to really understand ourselves. Sadly, our conditioned consciences will gravitate towards the crusade that keeps us in despair and segregated.

Dear Ego,

CHAPTER 25 - DESPAIR IN A WORLD OF WAR

The life-source inside can always feel the suffering of our conscious mind. Our unconscious wants to aide in vindicating that life is worth living in peace not war. Our self-love is the way out of our self-torture and anguish.

Dear Heart,
Our ego thrives on tormenting the heart, it is the bombing we inflict on ourselves every day, so the mind remains the powerful commander. The concept of life without anguish is worrisome.

Dear Ego,
Our life will always have adversity but the only way out of the challenge of life is by sitting with what arises. Holding space for our thoughts and loving what we feel. We need to be brave in our head space to let go of the hurts of life once we have felt them and accepted them. Being present in each moment will help us move through painful moments. We need each part of us to get through our carnage.

Dear Heart,
The division of self is all our reasoning knows. This part of us fears wholeness and believes our thinking mind will be abolished if we choose to move through strife together.

Dear Ego,
The division of self is nothing to fear and is part of our journey back home. On our divided path we learn to communicate with each other. Through the difficult communication we have with ourselves it leads us back home to ourselves.

26

Chapter 26 - Talk to Each Part of Ourselves with Gentle Loving Kindness

Dear Heart,

Embracing our heart and putting our guard down seems so frightening. Our ego does not know how to communicate with our heart.

Dear Ego,

Learning to talk to each part of ourselves is the evolution of the self. Starting by being gentle to us. Loving kindness will help bring the wall down that stands between us. With non-judgement we can both be the victors and end this war between us. Respecting ourselves and giving each side of us what we need is the truce our soul requires.

Dear Heart,

This mind of ours is selfish, it seeks pleasure at the expense of the heart. Our thoughts thrive when we break our own heart with words of dislike. Unkind words are the ideology of who we are, and our ID typically does not have any concern of what the heart needs.

Dear Ego,

Just talk to me instead of continuing to fight with me. Once we are in a loving relationship with each part of us, we can learn to compromise. Our heart desires a healthy relationship with the ego. It wants our thoughts to know, they are loved.

Dear Heart,

Words of shame, disgust and wrong doings hijack our mind. These horrible beliefs love tarnishing our heart. Words of war generate insecurity and doubt within. The fear of losing control of doubt stops us from talking gently to ourselves.

Dear Ego,

When our mind is hijacked, the heart will fight for us. It will whisper words of love and try to generate peace within all parts of us. Our peace is what will end the war.

Dear Heart,

Negative self-talk, disheartening words, and the belief we are not enough is the lifelong battle we know. It is a constant fight in our mind.

Dear Ego,

Listen to our heart. and let loving feelings consume our thoughts can help us find a middle ground. We can compromise to create a beautiful life in harmony and peace.

Dear Heart,

Our mind does not know how to listen or communicate what it needs. It is incapable of compromise and only knows how to self-serve.

Dear Ego,

Learning how to listen can be learnt. Start by, just listening to our heart whispers without judging it. Let our feelings arise and just observe them. To do this, our ego must let our heart in.

Dear Heart,

Our thoughts are reactive to what we feel, and they pull the trigger when threatened. We instantaneously defend against our feelings once the trigger is pulled. Our mind is fearful of our emotions and just attacks them instead of talking it out.

Dear Ego,

With practice and patience, we can slow down our racing defensive thoughts and listen to our intuition. When we are in a calm state of mind and not a war-torn state of being one can communicate with both parts of them self. Through observing each part of ourselves instead of being trigger happy by reactions, we can communicate with each other.

Dear Heart,

Living in a triggered state is what we know. We fight, we flight, we freeze. Communicating love is not in the vocabulary of the mind. The power of observation is native tongue.

Dear Ego,

The power of observation is the ability not to jump the gun on our reactions to our feelings that arise. It is about self-control and the ability to listen to what comes up for us. It is the strength filter through positive and negative emotions and helps reduce the stress in our mind and diminishes our negative emotions. This is the power of love.

Dear Heart,

Observation really does sound immensely powerful.

Dear Ego,

The power of observation is within us. Its strength aids us in heightening our awareness and the ability to focus our mind. Through the power of observation, we can be In tune with each other and give way to new behaviors and attitudes towards ourselves. It is the positive weapon that we can both utilize together and end our war. Our heart can observe our thoughts, and our ego can observe our feelings. Through the power of observation, we will have the ability to communicate our needs kindly to each other.

Dear Heart,

Shame and unworthiness are spoken in the mind. Does the heart really want this to communicate to our soul through the power of observation?

Dear Ego,

The heart longs to hear kind words and desires self-love but must process and love the thoughts that create our inner conflict. However, observation of our thoughts regardless of what they are can spark a conversation between ourselves and lead us into understanding why we think this way about ourselves. Our heart will always hold space for the feelings created by the mind's thoughts. It will beat softly in communicating and advocating for peace and love within.

Dear Heart,

Peace is a hard concept to learn when all we know is disturbance. Unlearning the raging war inside feels like an uphill battle with nothing on the other side of the hill.

Dear Ego,

Keeping faith that on the other side of the hill is freedom with a valley of tranquility. It is a place filled with self-love and respect. It is a state of being where we can both exist as our best version of us.

Dear Heart,

Faith is foreign to this part of us, especially while in a dismantled state. So please help our ego understand, does peace allow us to quiet the mind and exist in harmony?

Dear Ego,

Yes. It allows us to accept life in the moment and whatever may come our way. When one lives with peace in their heart, it does not mean that we will not live with hardship. Instead of waging war against the hardships and living stuck in despair, we can embrace them together. Our mind, body and soul are meant to be aligned as one. We are worthy of ourselves and worth becoming whole. Love for our unconscious parts exist and will never be dismissed. Our heart wants to take hold of our thoughts and hold them in a loving embrace because our soul knows the strength of our mind. We need all the ego's contributions to help us become conscious.

Dear Heart,

Our character does not believe we know how to connect. We are of the opinion that we are disassociated from everything. Even if we ponder the longing for connection, we do not know how to hold space for it. We are entrenched in a battle of our own shame and the cycle of shaming ourselves is the only thing we know.

Dear Ego,

We need connection to survive and our heart longs for it. The ego and the heart live parallel lives within us but to become whole we need to find a crossroad within ourselves so that we can have a whole relationship. Our peace will prevail once we end our shaming dual and truly know our worth.

Dear Heart,

We think that sounds lovely and well, peaceful, but how can we make a truce after a lifetime of suffering from the war wounds inflicted?

27

Chapter 27 - Embodying a Truce Within

Dear Ego,

Our soul never wanted the two selves to be at war with each other for so long. Our inner conflict was like the cold war. Accepting both parts of us our truce.

Dear Heart,

Breaking the patterns imprinted inside the trenches and ceasing fire will be difficult. Our ego will be triggered and will fire from time to time but in this moment our thoughts are calm. We have processed what acceptance can do for our state of being. We understand acceptance can bring peace and stop the persistent gun fire. It is our freedom from being a prisoner of our own war.

Dear Ego,

This shift in our mind has caused our heart to vibrate with love instead of shaking from bombs drop. Acceptance is the key to change and letting go of what hurts us. This little knowing of what acceptance can bring us is peace in our mind. Our heart is aware that life will continue to have diabolical forces presented from our mind. Influences of the outside world will continue to cause strife but if our mind can pause and observe these forced conditions, we are more open to accepting those hardships without being hard on ourselves. In the present moment we can free ourselves from our inner conflict. Accepting the truth about any given situation is our solitude and peace for the prisoners of war within in our hub.

Dear Heart,

Having a truce gives our mind mindfulness and the ability to vibrate high as well. Learning to listen to the loving words of wisdom from our heart will encourage the break stay from the argument in our head.

Dear Ego,

Healing trauma takes time, but it starts with love and will only heal with gentle loving kindness to us. The healing journey to come home to ourselves and be whole is worth the fight no matter the length of time at war. Our life's battles on our journey are meant to bring us to our truth and lead us to our authenticity.

Dear Heart,

Even after the war within has ended and the truce has been made, the effects of our trauma can last a lifetime. Some wars last years or even decades; we are sorry the story in our mind put us through so much added suffering and kept our bloodshed going for so long. Please accept our sincerest apology and help aid us in support our truce.

Dear Ego,

A loving heart always forgives, more importantly a loving center embraces the battle because our wisdom knows what will evolve from the war within ourselves. Our soul welcomes the truce with loving open arms. Our core looks forward to the day we can speak our truth together; mind, body, and soul.

Chapter 28 - Embracing Our Truth

Dear Heart,

Ego does not know what truth is, especially our own. Shortly after our birth our innocence and truth were replaced by stories and social conditioning. We quickly learned to believe and trust the outside world. We are now seeing the illusions of our world and what our inner world has to offer us.

Dear Ego,

Humankind are story tellers, because they want to mislead whoever will fall victim to the loss of innocence. Trusting what we are told and shown by the world is part of the journey. Born into an illusion to world where the division of self is meant to exist. Without the division created by the illusion there would be no journey or becoming whole. Hidden in the lies of the world is truth. One must endeavor darkness to find their truth among the world of illusion. With our open-mindedness we can disarm negative thoughts through the power of observation. Once disarmed and present we will stand as one.

Dear Heart,

Our thoughts are always armed and sadly, they tend to reject our truth. We only ever witnessed truth from a lying world that caused us to suffer immensely in a lifelong inner conflict. We hope to find our truth within. Through embracing each moment, we know we can detach from the lies and accept what is.

Dear Ego,

Attachment creates separation from us and in that division, violence is generated towards our authenticity. When we attach something outside of ourselves in the pursuit of happiness it tarnishes our inner sparkle. It devalues all of us, not just our heart. Instead of rejecting who we are and looking to others for joy, learn to value and accept all parts of who we are because this is our oneness.

Dear Heart,

Letting go of the weapons we think keep us safe in our bomb shelter seems unnerving but finding truth while trying to accept our truth while disarming ourselves is alarming. Although, it is something we think we desire.

Dear Ego,

Our nature is self-sabotaging when we must defend ourselves while armed. The guns in our head slowly destroy us with each shot fired leaving us feeling and thinking that we are incomplete. Accepting God's armor of love will make us whole and safe in our truce of truth.

Dear Heart,

Thinking we are incomplete is an innate part of us, we assume

CHAPTER 28 - EMBRACING OUR TRUTH

we lack the essentials to be whole. Believing in ourselves weighs heavily on the mind, like the weight of a canyon ball penetrating through an unknown victim.

Dear Ego,

Let us not make an ass out of you and me, our heart promises we are enough as we are. We will never be free from salvage until we accept all the fabrics of our life; mind and soul. Each part of us makes us whole. Accepting all of us will continue our treaty and allow us to stand together proudly in our authenticity. Remember once the canyon fires it lets go and becomes lighter.

Dear Heart,

The wise words I am observing and trying to understand are that of our truth and not defeat of the ego? It just means an end to the mind war?

Dear Ego,

Being authentic means knowing our values and holding value to them over what society thinks is valuable. It means believing in all parts of us. Once we really believe in our value, peace will come. Energy will flow back because the draining game of tug of war between the head and the heart will have ended. Know this as truth.

Dear Heart,

Accepting the undertaking of the heart's love within the concept of our mind seems difficult. Rationalizing how to love ourselves is illogical to the ID but wanting peace from our attacking thoughts is something our head space wants to accept and is perceived as calming.

Dear Ego,

Clasping onto our truth takes courage and tenacity. The choice to rise together is our truth and is ours to make. We can make it together or the ego can make the wrong decision again only to repeat the lessons of inner war again. We can remain bonded to our dark forces and limited belief system, or we can live by our own values, free from bondage.

Dear Heart,

All this time we thought of our mind as the marching soldiers protecting our thoughts and who we are. We are slowly grasping the concept that our current beliefs are slaves to the conditions of the outside world and not the warrior of our world within. Shifting our mindset will abolish the slavery we endure and encourage the inner warrior.

29

Chapter 29 - The Shift Within

Dear Ego,

All it takes is a shift in perspective to change the things we believe about ourselves and what we think is true.

Dear Heart,

Outside influences have hardened our perspective.

Dear Ego,

The outside influences are not present with us now, it is just us in our oneness. Becoming open minded and accepting of all perspectives is the bravery of the mind that will allow passage to the shift within. Our heart is always open and ready to embrace our thoughts as one.

Dear Heart,

Our ego is conditioned to know certainty and it fears the uncertainty of life. We are afraid to be receptive to all parts of us because our mind is rooted in fear and a shift requires our ego to be vulnerable.

Dear Ego,

Embracing vulnerability is the strength that will lead us to victory. It is receiving the light we hold within the darkness to create the certainty of who we are. Dark thoughts will always creep up because they are dark but being aware of them will allow us to look at them in a different light and replace them with positive thought in each moment.

Dear Heart,

Shedding light on the dark conversations we have been having in our mind for decades seems challenging but the desire to be loved in our entirety pushes us towards openness and allowing light to brighten our darkest moments.

Dear Ego,

The heart acknowledges that our light Smolders shortly after birth once the social conditioning begins in infancy. But the core of us is always light and love regardless of what we are trained to believe in combat. Our light is only submerged in darkness but is meant to be found. Life's journey is to endure adversity and lead us back to the light of passage and home to ourselves. Only once the mind shifts, can we find our way home.

Dear Heart,

We strongly believe that even once we let the light pass through, the darkness will come again.

Dear Ego,

My beloved, life is full of dark moments and even after the

shift, dark times will come again but when the dark night comes again, we will be aligned with one another and whole. When standing alongside one another it is much easier to find our light source again because we are no longer divided. In our wholeness we can trust ourselves and the light will shine with confidence during doomie days as it guides us together out of our gloom.

Dear Heart,

Starting to shift from our darkness to our light we will have to start with small steps, otherwise it might overwhelm our thoughts. A change in our defensive position and perspective will have to be one notion at a time.

Dear Ego,

Transcendence is a lifelong process and can only be completed by one belief at a time. Shifting to a new perspective is something the ego and mind can do in harmony, alongside the heart. We love that you want to change your position and evolve. The love we have within wants to evolve and be present in oneness with our thoughts.

Dear Heart,

Keep faith that the mind's focus is to shift alongside the heart to eventually merge with you. During this transition, please hold space for all our invaders and know that one day soon we will be united.

Dear Ego,

Our heart vows to hold space during your shift. It will love you during every shift you process.

30

Chapter 30 - Holding Space Until We Are Home

CHAPTER 30 - HOLDING SPACE UNTIL WE ARE HOME

Dear Heart,

It has been a drawn-out battle for both of us please render in the silence of space until this part of us returns home.

Dear Ego,

With love, you have our vow that our heart will hold space for this part of us, even if the attacks are present on the path home. Our light will shine on the dark paths while travelling home. Upon your arrival we will be whole.

Dear Heart,

The clash within has assaulted our heart but the ego marches towards the heart as peacekeepers now not as soldiers.

Dear Ego,

Our heart has been broken in combat, but love mends its wounds. Our soul seeks out the peacekeepers ready to have true joy, truth, and unconditional love. During the journey home remember our compassion is expansive.

Dear Heart,

Know this, we will end the inner dialog of war within our place of love, it will just take the veterans of war some time to disarm themselves.

Dear Ego,

Trust that we keep faith in our marching peacekeepers, we know they have come in love. There is always room for all entering the kingdom of love.

Dear Heart,

CHAPTER 30 - HOLDING SPACE UNTIL WE ARE HOME

Our troops coming home are grateful there is capacity in the kingdom of the heart. They know now true victory lies within loving all parts of us and they are excited to find their way back home.

Dear Ego,

No matter the pace of the marching thoughts, always remember all is welcomed in the heart's realm.

Dear Heart,

Slow and steady will lead us to our true state of being. Remain patient, we are coming home soon.

Dear Ego,

Know when you arrive, you will be embraced lovingly by the heart. Our heart will open the gate and our space within will let you enter your light.

Dear Heart,

Our war-torn veterans look forward to accepting the loving embrace and having peace of mind. once again.

31

Chapter 31 - Welcome Home

CHAPTER 31 - WELCOME HOME

Dear Ego,

Our Ego won some battles, but it did not win the war, love will always all concur and provide peace to the world of war. The newfound peace within brings the mind and heart in alignment. This alliance is our gateway to being whole and the discovery of our authentic self. Welcome home my love, we hope you find comfort in who you are.

Dear Heart,

Thank you for opening the gates as we arrived home to ourselves. After the decades of abuse we inflicted on the heart, our mind feared you would keep the gates locked and stand guard to keep us out.

Dear Ego,

Of course, the doors are always open. It was open the whole time because this is your home of comfort, compassion, empathy, joy, truth, and love. All we ever wanted was to be whole. When we are home, we are at peace and can live in a joyful state of being. Being open to the mind was our heart's salvation. Acceptance ends our war and allows the patterns of the mind to break and be replaced with gratitude.

Dear Heart,

This home feels safe and being in this state of being is much more pleasant than our state of war. For so long we feared becoming authentic we would lose this part of ourselves; rationale.

Dear Ego,

Being authentic does not mean our ego no longer exists.

CHAPTER 31 - WELCOME HOME

Our thoughts are always warranted, and they will always be validated from our heart when coming from a place of love. Being open just allows us to align our mind and heart. Letting our guard down makes space for both parts of us to exist as one. Our heart will always welcome you with open arms no matter what state of being we are in. Know you are needed and loved. Our heart wants to show you the gentle loving kindness we deserve. Trust that our softness is our strength and not the hardness of bullets.

Dear Heart,

With deepest sympathy we are sorry how many times we shot ourselves down. Our inner battle was neglectful to the ability to speak our truth, and it hardened us. Please know, it was what we knew but now we know different so we can be different. Know better do better.

Dear Ego,

Learning to love all parts of ourselves is the world war of a lifetime. Our inner battle is meant to bring us home to our riches. It is the life lesson through our hardships of self-trust and safety within. Our fight is our truth and being honest with ourselves. Speaking our truth is authentic and we cannot ever speak it until we win ourselves over in alignment with each other. My dear self, we forgive the bombs dropped on our hearts they were meant to explode so we could find the broken pieces and put them back together.

Dear Heart,

Thank you for kind words and encouragement, our tired army looks forward to our future at home together in one space.

Dear Ego,

Kindness is what the heart knows. With love we will nourish our worn-out veterans. In unity we will remain home and transcend further into enlightenment.

Dear Heart,

We deeply appreciate how much you have accepted us and welcomed us home given the amount of grief our thoughts have caused.

Dear Ego,

Remember in the land of love, you will always be accepted, it is unconditional. Our heart has been looking forward to the reunion since the day we divided. Welcome back, please stay forever because we have missed you.

Dear Heart,

We have been at war for so long we forgot what self-love feels like. We fired at words of admiration because we thought we were unworthy. We bombed love because we thought we were unlovable, how sad. We are sorry for the weapons used against our heart.

Dear Ego,

Love is forgiveness, and we forgive all the war tactics used against us. During the war, ego was still loved.

Dear Heart,

What a powerful thought knowing we were loved in our darkest moments. What a beautiful notion to know we were always welcomed home to our heart center.

CHAPTER 31 - WELCOME HOME

Dear Ego,

Always welcomed to your light and always loved.

Dear Heart,

Our ego puts the weapons used on the battlefield to rest and knows that war within has ended. We embrace ourselves and want to observe our thoughts with gentle loving kindness. We are at home and want to remain there as one.

Dear Ego,

Dear self, you are home, and you are unconditionally loved.

Printed in France by Amazon
Brétigny-sur-Orge, FR